THE EVERYTHING.

Memory Booster Puzzles Book

Dear Reader,

Has your memory been playing tricks on you? Then this book is for you! The puzzles in these pages will break your brain out of its normal routine by challenging it in novel ways.

I discovered the power of puzzles when I created Funster.com, a popular Web site with word games and other puzzles. Players at Funster.com can get seriously addicted to all of those small "aha!" moments that occur as puzzles are solved. Fortunately, a growing number of scientific studies indicate that puzzle solving is healthy and can improve one's memory.

This book is not designed for people who like to flaunt their high IQ! I work out at a health club, and most people there are just average folks who like to stay in shape by routinely exercising. Mental exercise is similar; we can keep our brain in shape by regularly challenging it with simple puzzles like the ones found in this book.

Children instinctively know that playing helps their brains grow. They play for fun, not for practical reasons. Puzzles are like that—they can help our brains continue to grow and keep our memories sharp while we have fun. Enjoy!

Charles Timmerman

THE
EVERYTHING.
MEMORY BOOSTER
PUZZLES
BOOK

The EVERYTHING® Series

Editorial

Director of Innovation	Paula Munier
Editorial Director	Laura M. Daly
Associate Copy Chief	Sheila Zwiebel
Acquisitions Editor	Lisa Laing
Production Editor	Casey Ebert

Production

Director of Manufacturing	Susan Beale
Production Project Manager	Michelle Roy Kelly
Prepress	Erick DaCosta Matt LeBlanc
Interior Layout	Heather Barrett Brewster Brownville Colleen Cunningham Jennifer Oliveira
Cover Design	Erin Alexander Stephanie Chrusz Frank Rivera

THE EVERYTHING.

MEMORY BOOSTER PUZZLES BOOK

Unforgettable puzzles to increase your brain power

Charles Timmerman
Founder of Funster.com

Avon, Massachusetts

For my father, Dave Timmerman.

An Everything® Series Book.
Everything® and everything.com® are registered trademarks of F+W Publications, Inc.

Published by Adams Media, an F+W Publications Company
57 Littlefield Street, Avon, MA 02322 U.S.A.
www.adamsmedia.com

ISBN-10: 1-59869-383-2
ISBN-13: 978-1-59869-383-6

Printed in the United States of America.

J   I   H   G   F   E

*This book is available at quantity discounts for bulk purchases.
For information, please call 1-800-289-0963.*

Contents

Acknowledgments

I would like to thank each and every one of the more than half a million people who have visited my Web site, *www.funster.com*, to play word games and puzzles. You have shown me how much fun puzzles can be and how addictive they can become!

It is always a pleasure to acknowledge my agent, Jacky Sach, whose help and expertise has been invaluable over the years.

Once again it was a delight working with everyone at Adams Media. I particularly want to thank my editor Lisa Laing, who provided the inspiration for this book.

I'm very fortunate to have Suzanne and Calla as a constant source of support and enthusiasm. Thanks for the memories!

Funster.com and What's in a Name? are trademarks of Charles Timmerman.

Introduction

▶ *Use it or lose it.* Everyone knows that physical exercise can keep our bodies healthy—just ask any of the millions of people who regularly visit a health club. New research tells us that we can also keep our brains fit with regular mental exercise. That's what this book is all about: mental aerobics that can give your memory a boost.

You don't have to be a "puzzle person" to enjoy this book. The puzzles here are made to engage your brain, not melt it down. It's similar to physical fitness where just walking can be beneficial; mountain climbing and marathon running are not required. The mental challenges here will lead you to those moments of creativity when your brain is perhaps building new pathways.

Why do we need to keep our brains mentally fit? Well, some people just want to confidently connect names to faces in social situations. Others want to reduce their number of "senior moments," a euphemism for episodes of forgetfulness, which can happen at any age. For all of us, mental agility is increasingly important to be successful in the world today. In this information age we need sharp brains to keep us afloat in a flood of data.

The good news is that scientific research suggests that mental aerobics can give our brains a boost. According to a study in the journal *Nature*, we can actually build brain mass by attempting mentally challenging tasks. In this study, volunteers spent three months learning to juggle (a mentally challenging task). Using MRI brain scans, it was discovered that the participants' brains had increased in volume. When the participants gave up juggling, their brains shrank back to their previous sizes. This book won't teach you how to juggle, but it will present you with numerous brain-building challenges.

Many people believe that memory loss is inevitable as we age. Research indicates that this doesn't have to be the case. In a study published in the *Journal of the American Medical Association*, 2,802 participants age 65 and older received cognitive training for two hours per week for five weeks. A significant number of the participants improved their memory and cognitive abilities, and this improvement persisted for two years after the training. Another study published in *The New England Journal of Medicine* found that people could reduce their risk of Alzheimer's disease by adding one mentally stimulating activity per week. Adding more activities, like working a crossword puzzle every day, was even better.

Research also points to lifestyle changes that can give your brain a boost. A healthy low-fat diet with lots of fruits and vegetables is important to keep your brain in peak condition. Staying physically fit benefits the brain as well as the rest of the body. And reducing stress will cut down on the mental wear and tear that keeps your mind from working efficiently. Doing all of these things, in addition to the mental aerobics in this book, can help give your memory a boost.

Motivation is important, so have fun as you start your training with these puzzles. Hopefully you will look forward to the challenges. There is a diversity of puzzles in this book, and some you will enjoy more than others. Give them all a chance—the ones that are the most frustrating at the start might become the most satisfying once they are mastered. It is OK to pick and choose from your favorites, but be sure to cross-train with a variety of puzzles for the most effective brain workout.

Your memory will work best if you have a positive, confident attitude. You can remember if you think you can! Getting this book and working these puzzles is a great start in boosting your memory.

Forget Me Nots

The puzzles in this chapter present a simple challenge: remember lists of random items. This might sound difficult at first, but it will become easy and fun when you use the link system. Perhaps you will discover secrets about how your memory works.

The Link System

The idea behind the link system is to make a mental chain out of the list of items to be remembered. This is done by associating each item in the list with the next item in some memorable way.

Example

Say we want to memorize this list of things:

- TREE
- WHEEL
- KNEE
- HOUSE
- HAT
- FERRY

To make our first link, we need to think of a mental image to associate TREE with WHEEL. This could be done by imagining a wheel sitting next to a tree—a logical choice, but not really a memorable one. Let your imagination go wild and think of a bunch of wheels racing up and down a tree like a racetrack. Or imagine a car with four trees in place of wheels (our imagination is not limited to only what is possible). These are things we would surely remember if we saw them in the real world. Actually "see" one of these images in your mind's eye. Now given TREE, you should think of WHEEL. The first link is made!

Here is the key: we remember unusual things, and we forget ordinary things. So the more remarkable, absurd, and bizarre you can make your link images, the better! Creating these weird associations is the fun part. Let's continue with our example.

Next on the list, we need to link WHEEL and KNEE. Maybe imagine a tattoo of a wheel being etched onto your knee (ouch). Or imagine a giant wheel balancing precariously on your knee. Pick the image that seems most absurd and actually visualize it in your mind.

To link KNEE and HOUSE we could imagine a giant's knee crashing through the roof of our house. We have put action into our association to make it memorable.

Next, we could link HOUSE with HAT by imagining a giant hat on a house. Or maybe imagine a thousand hats being thrown into the air by all of the houses in town. In this example, exaggeration makes the images stand-out. Imagine objects much bigger or more numerous than they really are.

For the last item in our example, we could link HAT with FERRY by imagining a ferry made from a giant hat. Or picture someone wearing a ferry as a hat! For this link, we have made an unforgettable image by interchanging the roles of the two items in an unusual way.

One more thing—we need to be able to remember the first item in this list, so let's link it to something relevant. We could associate our lists with this book. So in our example, TREE could be linked to this book by imagining a tree filled with copies of this book in place of leaves. Go ahead, pick a copy!

Tips

For a link to work best the items should interact with each other. Don't just imagine the two items sitting next to each other; they should actually *do* something with each other. Also, include lots of detail in your images to help lock the mental pictures into your memory.

Remember, you must actually *see* the images in your mind. Just thinking of great ideas for link associations is not enough; we have to really picture them. Go back through the example and take the time to see each association. Then close this book and run through the list, going from link to link. You might be surprised how easy it is.

The link system will work best for you when you come up with your own images. The creative act of dreaming up these associations will help cement them into your memory, and it will be a good mental exercise. No one else needs to know about the strange associations you create, so set your mind free and marvel at the bizarre images that will come forth! Children have no problem creating these kinds of silly pictures in their heads. With a little practice, your imagination will be back to where it was in grade school.

Forget Me Nots

Use the link system and create a memorable image for each neighboring pair. Vividly see each image in your mind's eye. As a check, immediately see if you can remember each item by running through all the links without looking. Then later in the day, or perhaps the next day, try to remember each item without looking at the list. You should even be able to run through a *Forget Me Not* list backwards by using the links in reverse. Almost like meditation, thinking through a *Forget Me Not* list can be relaxing!

You will probably get faster at memorizing the lists as you get more experienced associating word pairs. This is a good thing, and it shows that your mind is more able to focus. If you want, use a timer to see how fast you can memorize a list.

These *Forget Me Not* puzzles are not meant to be done all at once. After you remember a *Forget Me Not* list, work other puzzles in this book. Then return to this chapter and see if you can still remember the list. You might get better at the *Forget Me Not* lists as your brain gets a workout from the other puzzles in this book. For more of a challenge, see if you can remember two or more of these lists by linking them together.

Forget Me Not Challenge 1

chest	cushion
egg	cord
scissors	bucket
screw	roof
table	lock

- - - - - - - - - - - - - - - - - - - -

Forget Me Not Challenge 2

wheel	bird
plate	bottle
neck	train
kettle	pocket
heart	key

- - - - - - - - - - - - - - - - - - - -

Forget Me Not Challenge 3

worm	stick
hat	fish
head	band
shelf	leg
hook	nut

- - - - - - - - - - - - - - - - - - - -

Forget Me Not Challenge 1

_____	_____
_____	_____
_____	_____
_____	_____
_____	_____

- -

Forget Me Not Challenge 2

_____	_____
_____	_____
_____	_____
_____	_____
_____	_____

- -

Forget Me Not Challenge 3

_____	_____
_____	_____
_____	_____
_____	_____
_____	_____

- -

Forget Me Not Challenge 4

hospital	jewel
army	snake
stomach	sock
fly	umbrella
floor	leaf

Forget Me Not Challenge 5

needle	baby
shoe	wing
stamp	moon
map	engine
tooth	ship

Forget Me Not Challenge 6

hair	boy
cloud	monkey
bell	ring
pig	office
toe	pipe

Forget Me Not Challenge 4

_____   _____

_____   _____

_____   _____

_____   _____

_____   _____

- - - - - - - - - - - - - - - - - - - -

Forget Me Not Challenge 5

_____   _____

_____   _____

_____   _____

_____   _____

_____   _____

- - - - - - - - - - - - - - - - - - - -

Forget Me Not Challenge 6

_____   _____

_____   _____

_____   _____

_____   _____

_____   _____

- - - - - - - - - - - - - - - - - - - -

Forget Me Not Challenge 7

window	curtain
sun	dress
button	collar
bee	bone
bed	horse

- -

Forget Me Not Challenge 8

throat	book
foot	knife
drawer	pencil
camera	stem
sheep	library

- -

Forget Me Not Challenge 9

net	dog
pen	wire
arch	brick
finger	horn
receipt	tree

- -

Forget Me Not Challenge 7

_____   _____

_____   _____

_____   _____

_____   _____

_____   _____

- - - - - - - - - - - - - - - - - -

Forget Me Not Challenge 8

_____   _____

_____   _____

_____   _____

_____   _____

_____   _____

- - - - - - - - - - - - - - - - - -

Forget Me Not Challenge 9

_____   _____

_____   _____

_____   _____

_____   _____

_____

Forget Me Not Challenge 10

sail	line
ear	skin
card	nail
cake	tail
comb	flag

Forget Me Not Challenge 11

cow	lip
hammer	school
church	cart
box	muscle
match	bulb

Forget Me Not Challenge 12

bag	ball
pot	picture
hand	coat
knee	thread
bridge	boat

Forget Me Not Challenge 10

_____   _____

_____   _____

_____   _____

_____   _____

_____   _____

- -

Forget Me Not Challenge 11

_____   _____

_____   _____

_____   _____

_____   _____

_____   _____

- -

Forget Me Not Challenge 12

_____   _____

_____   _____

_____   _____

_____   _____

_____   _____

Forget Me Not Challenge 13

berry	spring
spoon	store
mouth	bath
chin	house
ticket	cat

- - - - - - - - - - - - - - - - - - -

Forget Me Not Challenge 14

wall	garden
ant	clock
blade	town
rail	cup
cheese	drain

- - - - - - - - - - - - - - - - - - -

Forget Me Not Challenge 15

whistle	eye
brain	arm
shirt	carriage
sponge	star
rat	feather

- - - - - - - - - - - - - - - - - - -

Forget Me Not Challenge 13

_____	_____
_____	_____
_____	_____
_____	_____
_____	_____

- - - - - - - - - - - - - - -

Forget Me Not Challenge 14

_____	_____
_____	_____
_____	_____
_____	_____
_____	_____

- - - - - - - - - - - - - - -

Forget Me Not Challenge 15

_____	_____
_____	_____
_____	_____
_____	_____
_____	

Forget Me Not Challenge 16

basket	brush
thumb	glove
face	door
skirt	tongue
oven	root

- - - - - - - - - - - - - - - -

Forget Me Not Challenge 16

_____   _____

_____   _____

_____   _____

_____   _____

_____   _____

2

Crossword Puzzles

Studies have shown that doing crossword puzzles is a great way to keep your brain young. Give the puzzles in this chapter your best shot. It's okay if you can't fill in every entry; you will still be getting a good mental workout.

Crossword Puzzle 1

ACROSS

1. Prefix with red or structure
4. __-Wan Kenobi
7. Clinton's attorney general
8. Reject
10. Poison
11. Washington bills
12. Public spat
13. Map within a map
17. Past pudgy
18. Former spouses
20. Light bulb unit
22. Coral formation
24. "A mouse!"
26. Roll call response
29. 500 sheets
31. Bert's Muppet pal
32. Doctors' org.
33. Wound up
35. Actress Zellweger
37. ___-garde
38. Nike's swoosh, e.g.
39. Ocean motion
41. Narcissist's love
42. Get-up-and-go

DOWN

2. Supermodel Campbell
3. Golfer Palmer, informally
4. Lennon's love
5. ___ fide
6. Crude cartel
9. Where the deer and the antelope play
14. Place to build
15. Chewy candy
16. Wish granter
18. Raring to go
19. Total
20. Part of WWW
21. Have a go at
23. Spooky
25. Actress Winslet
27. Christopher of "Superman"
28. Panoramic view
30. Track event
32. Book of maps
34. Down in the dumps
35. It's over your head
36. Billionth: Prefix
40. "__ had it up to here!"

Solution on page 142

Crossword Puzzle 2

ACROSS

1. Japanese wrestling
3. Singleton
5. Rarer than rare
7. Pied Piper follower
8. Picture puzzle
9. Kind of lily
12. Custard dessert
13. Abduct
16. Actor Neeson
19. Artist Matisse
20. Turn away
21. Balloon filler
23. Bar bill
24. Proposer's prop
25. Marathoner's staying power
28. Short snooze
30. Bother
31. Bangkok native
33. Put in stitches
36. Fashionably nostalgic
37. "Big" London landmark
38. Mad Hatter's drink
39. Chip dip
40. Supreme Diana
41. Pancake topper

DOWN

1. T-bone, e.g.
2. Director Welles
3. Hooter
4. Mayberry's town drunk
6. Jazzy Fitzgerald
7. Sought office
10. In flames
11. "Raging Bull" subject
14. Thickheaded
15. Assumed name
17. Nose-in-the-air type
18. ___ Lee cakes
19. Clue
22. ___-bitsy
26. ___ Dame
27. "___ takers?"
28. ___ King Cole
29. Buenos ___
30. Wonderment
32. Get wind of
34. Online auctioneer
35. "2001" computer
38. Tic-___-toe

Solution on page 142

Crossword Puzzle 3

ACROSS

1. Author Fleming
3. "You betcha!"
5. Source of iron
7. Idaho's capital
8. Swashbuckler Flynn
10. Sister of Zsa Zsa
12. Chicken ___ king
13. "___ Haw"
15. Dress down
19. "Dancing Queen" quartet
20. Actress Russo
21. Macaroni shape
23. Stick up
24. Form 1040 issuer
25. Lyricist Gershwin
27. Beast of burden
29. Noodles
33. Golden rule preposition
34. Sling mud at
35. Take a load off
36. Chest material
40. Furthermore
42. "Much ___ About Nothing"
43. King Kong, e.g.
45. Climber's goal
46. Dressed to the ___
47. Fork over
48. ___ kwon do

DOWN

1. Cut off
2. It smells
4. Deadly virus
6. Gun, as an engine
8. Hot coal
9. Steak order
11. Arthur of "The Golden Girls"
13. "The Sopranos" network
14. Flow's partner
16. Trap
17. ___ Lilly & Co.
18. Seashore
19. Location of Bill Clinton's Hope
20. Washer cycle
22. Muffin choice
26. Photo ___ (media events)
28. Beaver, to Ward
30. Aviator Earhart
31. Snack in a shell
32. Band aide
37. Comedian Carvey
38. Director Howard
39. Tank filler
40. Sound booster
41. Hog haven
44. Electric fish

Solution on page 142

Crossword Puzzle 4

ACROSS

2. Dove's sound
3. Put in the hold
6. Sharpen
7. Land measure
11. Come to terms
12. Try out
14. Big brass horn
15. Egyptian boy king
16. Soothing ointment
18. Wray of "King Kong"
19. Earring site
21. Mary ___ cosmetics
22. Sierra Nevada resort
25. Prohibition
26. Rocker John
28. Scored 100 on
31. Foxx of "Sanford and Son"
33. Alma ___
34. Prefix with physics or physical
37. Low digits
38. "i" completer
39. Prepared
40. Gymnast Comaneci
41. West Pointer

DOWN

1. Close
2. Penny
4. ___ Haute, Ind.
5. Small songbird
8. Discontinue
9. ___ of Sandwich
10. Car
13. Do in, as a dragon
14. Oklahoma city
17. MasterCard rival

18. Deadly
20. Sis's sib
22. Basic belief
23. Ranch worker
24. Checkup
25. Sugar source
26. Prepare for publication
27. Miners' finds
29. Egypt's capital
30. ___ vu
32. Pops

34. Honey drink
35. Leave speechless
36. Jekyll's alter ego

Solution on page 142

Crossword Puzzle 5

ACROSS

1. Nets
3. Egg ___ yung
6. Martini garnish
8. Shoe bottom
10. Puerto ___
12. Hatchling's home
16. Fat in a can
18. Brewer's need
20. Use a swizzle stick
22. Walkie-talkie word
23. Inquire
25. Waste maker
27. Got wind of
28. "Full Metal Jacket" setting, for short
30. Japanese cartoon art
33. Back talk
34. "Alley ___!"
35. Take in or let out
37. Fall from grace
38. Vintner's vessel
39. Writer Hemingway
41. Tropical weather disturbance
42. Kyoto cash

DOWN

1. American ___, Massachusetts state tree
2. Burn the surface of
3. Elevator stop
4. Black gold
5. Baker's need
6. Academy Awards
7. "La Dolce ___"
9. Dripping
11. Homeric epic
13. Needle hole
14. Tranquil
15. Bills
17. Buck's mate
19. Fraud
21. Flourish
24. Hang on to
26. Hiker's path
29. Excuse
31. Telegraph code name
32. Exhausted
34. Unseat
36. Short and to the point
38. Tape player
40. Like a wallflower

Solution on page 142

Crossword Puzzle 6

ACROSS

2. Feel sorry for
6. Bean curd product
8. Paid player
9. California's Big ___
11. "Star Wars" sage
13. Can't stand
15. Business abbr.
16. Spelling contest
17. Gymnast Korbut
18. Enormous
21. Freezer cubes
22. Not together
25. Track down
27. "Terrible" czar
28. Art ___ (retro style)
31. Rotten
32. Shah's land, once
35. Betty of cartoons
37. Think the world of
38. "Sophie's Choice" Oscar winner
39. Wrestling surface
41. Way in or out
43. Yarns
44. Cantankerous
45. Wrapped up

DOWN

1. Dough dispenser?
2. Cut back
3. Pucker-producing
4. Numero ___
5. Enemy
7. Take advantage of
8. Cure-all
10. Four Corners state
12. Finger or toe
13. Dover's state: Abbr.
14. Wise guy
16. Get-out-of-jail money
17. Gumbo veggie
19. Secondhand
20. Cast-of-thousands film
23. Steer clear of
24. Egypt's Sadat
26. Go with the flow
29. Narrow opening
30. Hoops grp.
31. Head honcho
33. Highways and byways
34. Nautilus captain
36. Southpaw
37. IMac maker
40. Like the Sahara
42. Pea's place

Solution on page 142

Crossword Puzzle 7

ACROSS

1. Actress Witherspoon
3. "___ the season . . ."
7. Public square
9. Monopoly payment
11. Tell a whopper
13. Celestial hunter
14. Frank
16. Canyon comeback
18. ___ New Guinea
22. Bring together
24. Gofer's job
25. Once around the track
27. Actor Baldwin
28. South Carolina's capital
31. Wager
32. Precedes maiden name
33. Artist's stand
36. Tennis great Arthur
39. Gallery display
40. Neckline shape
41. Itsy-bitsy
42. Ginger ___
43. By way of
44. Leary's drug
45. Saddam ___

DOWN

1. Eminem's genre
2. Mall binge
4. Go bad
5. Conceited
6. Buddy
8. Office note
10. Transport to Oz
12. Be in the red
15. California wine valley
17. Special-occasion dishes
18. Opposite of post-
19. Esoteric
20. ___ Sam
21. Winter ailment
22. Optimistic
23. Guitarist Clapton
24. Pass, as time
26. The color of honey
29. Zodiac lion
30. Part of T.G.I.F.
34. Devil's doings
35. Minimum
36. Not home
37. Make well
38. Porgy's woman
39. Diarist Frank
42. Volcanic spew

Solution on page 143

Crossword Puzzle 8

ACROSS

1. Bucks and does
5. Reunion attendee
8. Jeans material
9. Phi ___ Kappa
10. Oregon's capital
12. Border
13. Prefix with cycle or sex
14. Sharon of Israel
15. Garr of "Tootsie"
16. ___ up (come clean)
17. Go kaput
19. Vote in
22. Pepper's partner
23. Bin ___
25. Come to pass
28. British john
29. Reebok rival
31. Days of ___
33. 100 centavos
35. Make amends (for)
37. Explosive letters
38. Actor Sharif
39. Track shape
40. Final Four game
41. NASDAQ debut
43. Coffee, slangily
44. "Nova" network
45. Poke fun at
46. "___, humbug!"

DOWN

2. Genesis locale
3. Send, as payment
4. Texas Panhandle city
5. Consumed
6. Soup scoop
7. Press Secretary DeeDee ____
9. Parting word
10. Hourglass contents
11. Tackle box item
14. Length times width
18. Ice house
20. And so on: Abbr.
21. Seaquake consequence
22. Scissors sound
24. Major artery
26. Meter maid of song
27. Barbie's beau
28. Disinfectant brand
30. "M*A*S*H" setting
32. Sign up
34. Sea plea
36. Poet Pound
38. Prophetic signs
42. Egg cells
43. Triangular sail

Solution on page 143

Crossword Puzzle 9

ACROSS

3. Guys' partners
5. Scout unit
6. Ground breaker
8. Nick at ___
9. Plot
12. Sprite
13. Change, as the Constitution
16. Irene of "Fame"
17. Actress Moore
19. Kind of bean
20. Winter fall
21. String quartet member
24. Pot top
26. Thinly spread
28. Shakespearean king
30. Have a bawl
31. Lend a hand
32. To and ___
33. Decay
34. Musical chairs goal
36. ___ Aviv
37. Katmandu's land
38. Pull the plug on

DOWN

1. Geyser output
2. Alpine call
3. ___-Xers (boomers' kids)
4. Took to court
6. "Where the heart is"
7. Blacken
10. Internet letters
11. Wraps up
12. Author Jong
14. Bear lair
15. Fuzzy fruit
16. Shoreline recess
18. Back tooth
22. Eye up and down
23. Quickly, in memos
25. Clothesline alternative
27. River of Hades
29. Chosen few
30. Gear tooth
31. Tint
32. Kismet
33. Caboose
34. Like a fox
35. Raggedy doll

Solution on page 143

Crossword Puzzle 10

ACROSS

4. Appear to be
6. Polynesian carving
7. Wheel shaft
9. Apollo destination
10. Shell game, e.g.
12. Part of CNN
13. Fortune-teller's card
15. Respond to reveille
17. Light bulb, in comics
19. Playing marble
20. ___ d'oeuvre
21. Weaving machine
23. Simple
25. Part to play
26. Unwanted e-mail
28. Loch ___
30. It may be checkered
32. "___ Well That Ends Well"
33. In ___ straits
34. Trade
35. ___ Mahal
36. Cacophony
37. Soccer legend

DOWN

1. Office fill-in
2. Cloud number
3. Snake sound
5. Photo finish
6. Cereal box tiger
8. Enticed
11. Indian corn
14. "___ the night before . . ."
15. Accumulate
16. Flower holder
17. Composer Stravinsky
18. Bloke
21. True-blue
22. "___ Lisa"
24. Cain's brother
26. Shoe material
27. Open a crack
29. Pan-fry
31. "The final frontier"

Solution on page 143

Crossword Puzzle 11

ACROSS

2. Rock's Bon ___
3. Run in neutral
6. ___-Mart
7. Squirrel away
11. One of the Three Bears
13. Cast out
15. Scent
16. Consumed
18. Stubble remover
20. Accord maker
24. Fly like an eagle
25. Hairless
27. Stir-fry pan
28. Utopian
29. Take care of
31. ___ Strauss & Co.
32. Singer Turner
33. Party handout
34. Carnival city
35. Yo-Yo Ma's instrument
36. Lose traction

DOWN

1. Thunder sound
2. Holy war
4. Sandwich shop
5. Out of this world
8. Broadcast
9. Letter starter
10. Paraphernalia
12. Ritzy
14. Ponce de ___
17. Urged (___ on)
19. Unescorted
21. Lasso loop
22. Sharp-smelling
23. Bullwinkle, for one
25. Britain's Tony
26. Kind of eclipse
29. Fork prong
30. Pueblo material
31. Fibber
32. Clock sound with tick
33. Henhouse raider

Solution on page 143

Crossword Puzzle 12

ACROSS

2. Mao ___ tung
5. Take five
8. Wild blue yonder
10. Ready for business
13. Make into law
15. ___ out a living
17. Go it alone
18. ___ Solo of "Star Wars"
19. Call on
20. Part of UNLV
22. __ sapiens
25. Love, Italian-style
28. Storm preceder
30. No-win situation
31. Least costly
33. Clear the blackboard
35. Sagan of "Cosmos"
36. ___ Beta Kappa
38. "__ we there yet?"
39. Singer Cara
40. "Tickle me" Muppet doll
42. Venus de ___
44. Pop singer Tori
45. Costa ___
47. Long ___ and far away
48. Vintage
49. Medicine-approving org.
50. ___ Baba

DOWN

1. Mass __
3. Take to court
4. Atlantis, Endeavor, or Discovery, e.g.
6. Beach souvenir
7. ___ Ness monster
9. Ukraine's capital
11. School org.
12. ___ Moines
14. Ark builder
16. Fate
21. World Cup sport
23. ___-jongg
24. Grand ___ Opry
25. Bridal path
26. Loaded
27. Soccer star Hamm
29. PC alternative
30. Intense fear
32. Jack and Jill's vessel
33. Adam's madam
34. __ Paulo, Brazil
36. Praline nut
37. Baghdad resident
41. Fall behind
42. Cattle call?
43. ___ of Man
44. Tack on
46. Under the weather

Solution on page 143

Crossword Puzzle 13

ACROSS

1. Bottomless pit
6. Snake charmer's snake
7. Thailand, once
8. Pay tribute to
9. Wrinkle remover
10. Paul Bunyan's tool
11. CD-___
12. "Star Wars" director
17. Tarzan's transport
18. Headed for overtime
19. Uncle ___
21. Urban haze
23. Salty sauce
25. Tuckered out
27. Slugger Williams
28. Eat away at
29. Cub Scout groups
30. Opening for a coin
33. Artist Picasso
35. Quote
36. Relocate
37. Window ledge
38. Field yield
39. Iowa State city

DOWN

1. Tummy trouble
2. Beat it
3. Up to the job
4. Japanese verse
5. Tonic's partner
7. Soft drink
11. ___ Tin Tin
13. Diet guru Jenny
14. Transmits
15. Foe
16. Hertz competitor
18. Dog in Oz
20. Concert venue
21. Witnessed
22. Red planet
24. Nabisco cookie
26. "___ we forget . . ."
29. ___ Perignon
31. Not as much
32. Scrabble piece
34. Life story, for short

Solution on page 144

Crossword Puzzle 14

ACROSS

1. Narcotic
6. Leave out
8. Alias letters
9. Neptune's domain
10. FedEx alternative
11. She sheep
14. Nebraska city
16. The yoke's on them
18. Chinese Chairman
20. Director's cry
24. Clearasil target
25. Home to Denali National Park
26. Intended
28. Massage with the hands
30. Spartan
32. Cheshire Cat feature
33. Singer Tucker
34. Chow down
35. Blender setting to reduce to mush
36. Fairy tale starter
37. Pay-___-view

DOWN

2. Baseball is our national one
3. Eisenhower nickname
4. Motorists' org.
5. Outfit
7. Bar
12. John Lennon hit
13. Precise
15. Bumpkin
17. Long, long time
19. River in a Strauss waltz
20. Liability's opposite
21. Spoken for
22. Alpha's opposite
23. At hand
27. French farewell
29. Went out with
31. Parade spoiler
35. "The Raven" poet

Solution on page 144

Crossword Puzzle 15

ACROSS

1. Part of UCLA
4. It'll keep you warm in the winter
7. Actress Thurman
9. Low in fat
10. "If all __ fails . . ."
11. Vaughan of jazz
13. Back talk
15. Em, to Dorothy
16. Something to lend or bend
17. ___ firma
19. An amoeba has one
20. ___ Gras
22. Bar order, with "the"
23. Cheney's predecessor
24. Crock
26. On the ball
28. "__ to Joy"
29. Debtor's letters
30. Hoover, for one
32. Pageant crown
34. ___ spumante
35. Hanker for

DOWN

2. ___ Na Na
3. Kick off
5. Guarantee
6. Run through
7. Gorbachev's nation
8. ___ culpa
9. Detest
12. Not digital
14. Practice boxing
15. St. Louis landmark
18. ___ colada
20. Syrup flavor
21. Burn balm
22. WWW address
25. Prefix with cycle or focal
26. Fess up
27. "Mazel ___!"
28. Quaker ___
31. Mayberry boy
33. Lend a hand

Solution on page 144

Crossword Puzzle 16

ACROSS

3. Townshend of The Who
5. Gun rights org.
7. Penned
9. Activities on eBay
11. Answer to a charge
12. Came to
13. False god
15. Edison's middle name
18. Took a load off
20. Composer Copland
22. Mrs. Bush
24. Broom __ (comics witch)
26. Former Russian space station
27. Shake up
31. Tune out
33. HI Hi
36. Feline line
37. Resistance to change
38. Dig like a pig
39. Tied

DOWN

1. Mexicali Miss
2. Sister of Venus Williams
3. Tempo
4. Astronaut Grissom
5. It might be found in a ring
6. Govern
8. Mojavi Desert AFB
10. Places for prices
14. Lord's Prayer start
16. Place to hibernate
17. Actor Kilmer
19. Assert without proof
21. Inauguration Day recital
23. Actress Jolie
24. She was named after Mt. Everest climber?
25. Historical period
28. Peru's capital
29. Stranded motorist's need
30. The Buckeye State
32. Memo
34. Prefix with lock or knock
35. ___ Lanka

Solution on page 144

Crossword Puzzle 17

ACROSS

3. Gawk
5. Gratis
7. Horn sound
8. Funeral song
10. Bona ___
12. Stink
13. Mea ___
17. Threesome
18. Luau dance
19. In the know
22. ___ Carlo
23. Mary Kay competitor
25. Swiss peaks
27. Nothing more than
28. Preschooler
30. Fritter away
32. Bluegrass instrument
34. Gymnast's goal
35. Relatives
36. Graph line
37. Entice
38. V-formation fliers

DOWN

1. Room at the top
2. Monopoly buy
4. Artist Warhol
5. Run away
6. Conjure up
9. Actress Garbo
11. Twofold
14. Molecule part
15. Paint layer
16. Bundle or arrows
20. Put on
21. Sunrise direction
24. Paddles
26. Letterman rival
29. Warning sign
30. Withdraw gradually
31. To-do list item
32. "___ there, done that"
33. Stick (out)
34. Newsweek alternative

Solution on page 144

3

Sudoku Puzzles

Sudoku burst onto the world stage in 2005 and continues to grow in popularity. Perhaps one of the secrets to its success is the puzzle's charming simplicity. Sudoku is played on a 9x9 grid. Heavier lines subdivide this grid into nine 3x3 boxes. The object is to fill in the grid so that every row, column, and 3x3 box contains the numbers one through nine with no repeats. The puzzle begins with some of the numbers already entered. There will always be only one solution for each puzzle.

Sudoku Puzzle 1

8			7	1	5			4
		5	3			6	7	
3		6	4		8	9		1
	6			5			4	
			8		7			
	5			4			9	
6		9	5		3	4		2
	4	9		2	5			
5			1	6	4			9

Solution on page 145

Sudoku Puzzle 2

3	4		8	2	6		7	1
		8				9		
7	6			9			4	3
	8		1		2		3	
	3						9	
	7		9		4		1	
8	2			4			5	9
		7				3		
4	1		3	8	9		6	2

Solution on page 145

9	2		4		6		7	1
			9	3	7			
7				1				5
1	7		8		5		4	6
			1		2			
4	9		7		3		2	8
5				2				7
			6	8	1			
3	1		5		9		8	4

Solution on page 145

	1	6		2		4	9	
7		9		6		2		5
8	4			9			6	3
		4		7		5		
			2		6			
		1		5		8		
4	8			3			1	2
6		3		1		7		8
	2	5		8		9	3	

Solution on page 145

Sudoku Puzzle 5

		9	8	7	5	2		
	4			3		5		
3	5					9		7
1			9	4	2			8
			7	1	3			
4			5	8	6			2
5	2					8		4
	8			9		1		
	1		3	5	8	7		

Solution on page 145

Sudoku Puzzle 6

		7	9	6	2	4		
9				1				2
	1		8	5	3		6	
5			4	7	9			1
				8				
4			3	2	1			7
	9		2	4	8		5	
6				3				8
		8	6	9	5	1		

Solution on page 145

Sudoku Puzzle 7

1			3	7	6			4
7								5
6		8	4	5	1	3		9
			7	6	9			
		3		2		8		
			1	3	8			
4		1	6	8	7	5		2
3								6
5			9	1	3			8

Solution on page 146

Sudoku Puzzle 8

9			2		7		5	
6	2					3	1	
	8					4		
4	3		7	8	1	2	6	
	6			4		9		
1	5		9	2	6	8	3	
	7					5		
3	9					7	8	
5			8		9	2		

Solution on page 146

Sudoku Puzzle 9

1		8	4	6	3	7		9
				2				
2			1		8			3
5	6		7		4		3	8
				1				
7	1		3		2		6	4
6			8		9			5
				5				
8		5	2	4	7	6		1

Solution on page 146

Sudoku Puzzle 10

	3	5	9	2	4	1	7	
		2	3	8	7	6		
5		1		6		2		7
		7		4		8		
3		6		9		5		1
		3	4	5	6	9		
	5	8	1	7	9	4	3	

Solution on page 146

Sudoku Puzzle 11

		9	5	4	1	8		
				3				
4	8						5	1
5	3		1	9	2		8	6
			6	7	3			
7	2		4	5	8		3	9
3	6						1	5
				1				
		1	3	2	5	4		

Solution on page 146

Sudoku Puzzle 12

1			2		5			8
9	4						2	5
7	5			9			3	6
	7		4	1	6		8	
	8						5	
	1		5	3	8		4	
5	3			6			9	2
8	2						6	4
6			7		2			3

Solution on page 146

	5	4				8	3	
1				6				7
7	8		2	3	5		4	6
	2	7				4	6	
				9				
	6	3				9	1	
2	7		1	4	6		8	9
3				2				4
	9	6				2	5	

Solution on page 147

5	3		2	9	6		8	7
		4		8		6		
			4		5			
4	7			3			2	6
		2		6		5		
6	1			2			3	9
			6		3			
		7		5		9		
1	4		8	7	9		6	5

Solution on page 147

1	9		7		5		6	3
		7	4		6	5		
	2	5				4	7	
8		6		5		7		9
5		2		3		1		6
	6	3				9	8	
		8	3		2	6		
7	5		6		8		1	2

Solution on page 147

Sudoku Puzzle 16

5		7	2	4	1	3		6
	6		5		9		7	
3								4
		6		2		7		
	2		7	9	3		6	
		8		5		4		
8								1
	4		3		5		8	
1		5	4	7	8	6		2

Solution on page 147

4		2	6		5	3		9
		7		4		2		
9			7		3			1
8				1				6
		4	3	5	2	1		
3				6				4
5			2		4			3
		8		3		9		
2		3	1		8	6		7

Solution on page 147

		3	9		4	6		
	8		2	1	7		9	
9			8	6	3			4
	9						6	
		7	6	2	1	3		
	6						1	
5			7	3	6			1
	7		4	8	2		3	
		8	1		5	7		

Solution on page 147

Sudoku Puzzle 19

1	8		9		2		3	7
	7						9	
6			8	3	7			4
2	4						6	9
		5	4		9	2		
7	9						5	8
8			6	7	1			3
	3						2	
4	1		2		3		8	5

Solution on page 148

			3	2	6			
		1	7		8	4		
	8	5		1		3	6	
5	6			7			4	1
			8	6	4			
7	2			9			8	3
	1	9		4		7	5	
		2	9		7	1		
			5	3	1			

Solution on page 148

		3	1			8		
2				6				3
6	9			5			2	1
7		6	1	8	4	3		2
			2		5			
1		2	3	9	6	5		7
8	2			3			7	9
9				4				6
		4		2		1		

Solution on page 148

Sudoku Puzzle 22

	8		5	3	2		4	
4				6				1
2	3		4		7		5	8
6	5						7	3
			3		5			
3	9						1	5
9	6		2		3		8	7
7				4				9
	2		7	9	1		6	

Solution on page 148

2	6	7	5		1	4	9	3
1								2
9			7		2			8
	5	3				2	8	
				4				
	9	1				6	4	
7			8		6			5
5								6
3	8	6	2		7	9	1	4

Solution on page 148

Sudoku Puzzle 24

7	1						6	8
		9	8		4	5		
	4						3	
	7	6		4		8	5	
	5	3	6	8	1	7		9
	2	8		3		6		4
	3						2	
		4	1		9	3		
6	9						8	4

Solution on page 148

Sudoku Puzzle 25

	5	9	4		1	8	7	
4			3		8			1
1								4
	1		5		7		6	
	8		2	3	4		5	
	4		8		6		3	
8								6
5			6		3			9
	6	1	7		9	2	8	

Solution on page 149

Sudoku Puzzle 26

	6		7	1	5		2	
			2		4			
7			3	8	9			5
2			5	4	1			8
		9		3		5		
1			9	2	8			6
5			1	9	2			7
			4		3			
	9		8	5	6		3	

Solution on page 149

Sudoku Puzzle 27

1		8				3		6
			5	3	2			
	3		6		8		7	
	1	3	4	7	6	2	8	
		2				7		
	7	4	3	2	5	6	9	
	8		9		4		6	
			2	6	7			
4		5				9		7

Solution on page 149

	1		3		2		9	
8			1		7			6
	4			8			7	
	3		9	6	8		5	
	2	4	7		1	6	8	
	8		2	5	4		3	
	7			1			6	
2			4		9			5
	9		6		5		4	

Solution on page 149

	4	5	8	3	1	6	9	
	6	3		2		7	5	
2				7				4
			2	6	5			
		6				8		
			1	8	4			
3				1				7
	7	1		4		5	8	
	8	4	6	5	7	2	1	

Solution on page 149

	8			1			5	
	6	5		9		4	7	
		9	5	6	2	8		
5		7				6		1
		4		3		2		
9		8				7		5
		2	1	4	9	3		
	4	6		5		1	8	
	9			7			2	

Solution on page 149

	1		9	3	4		5	
	8						4	
9				5				1
1	6	5				4	3	7
		7	4	1	5	6		
4	2	8				5	1	9
6				4				2
	7						6	
	3		7	9	6		8	

Solution on page 150

Sudoku Puzzle 32

	4	5	6		3	7	8	
6								9
	8		4		2		6	
7		6	5		9	3		8
	1						9	
5		8	3		1	4		7
	6		1		4		5	
1								6
	7	2	9		6	1	3	

Solution on page 150

5	9	6	2	1	7	3	8	4
			4		9			
		4				2		
4	6						2	8
	5	2				1	4	
8	1						5	3
		5				4		
			6		8			
7	4	3	1	9	5	8	6	2

Solution on page 150

4

Word Search Puzzles

All of these word search puzzles are in the traditional format. Words are hidden in a grid of letters in any direction: horizontal, vertical, diagonal, forward, or backward. Words can overlap. For example, the letters at the end of the word "MAST" could be used as the start of the word "STERN." Only the letters A to Z are used, and any spaces in an entry are removed. For example, "TROPICAL FISH" would be found in the grid as "TROPICALFISH."

Countries

```
R N D O X P M A L A Y S I A I R E B I L
H A N G O L A F Y U G O S L A V I A G K
R T G O A L S X I H X N O R W A Y A E T
D U H T B I V S L N P E U F A D N A W R
E H A A M J R L B O L S M Z I Z E P L N
N B N I R I S A R X E A N B L X T N I K
M I A K L G O T G L I O N E O V H X T J
A G I A X H U X L L R X Y D G U E U H V
R U N V U G T E A T U M U R N Y R S U S
K K D O A Z H M H V U B P E O K L G A G
A R O L L C K K O I I S W V M Z A E N T
I K N S Y M O D G N I K D E T I N U I T
B U E E P R R L D N A I N P B A D U A Y
I O S J E Z E I G B I I N A D U S K R W
M B I A Y B A A O C S W P C U X Z R R Q
A D A H C X P K R T J C R O A T I A O N
N C O N G O D N A L R E Z T I W S I D O
E C E E R G O N I R A M N A S H E N N S
C D S E V I D L A M A I S I N U T E A H
I B U N D A Y I V F V X O H T O S E L N
```

ALBANIA
ANDORRA
ANGOLA
BELGIUM
BHUTAN
BULGARIA
CAPE VERDE
CHAD
CONGO
CROATIA
DENMARK

ETHIOPIA
FINLAND
GHANA
GREECE
INDIA
INDONESIA
LESOTHO
LIBERIA
LITHUANIA
LUXEMBOURG
MALAYSIA
MALDIVES

MALI
MONGOLIA
NAMIBIA
NETHERLANDS
NORTH KOREA
NORWAY
PORTUGAL
RWANDA
SAN MARINO
SEYCHELLES
SINGAPORE
SLOVAKIA

SOUTH KOREA
SRI LANKA
SUDAN
SWITZERLAND
TOGO
TUNISIA
TURKMENISTAN
UKRAINE
UNITED KINGDOM
YUGOSLAVIA

Solution on page 150

United States

```
I T N A G I H C I M H A W A I I S T N W
L O K R O Y W E N S M S A X E T B N E T
O F W K P A N I L O R A C H T U O S E N
U Z L A X Y D E L A W A R E O R T A S Y
I G A N O Z I R A W S X S D T V N S S U
S M I S S O U R I H J U A H I H E N E H
I D N A L S I E D O H R C R P M B A N C
A P N S N K S U H C O A G A P A R K N M
N T C E E G T I A L R I L N I T A F E J
A E O Y W A O S O O N L N A S O S W T S
M N N K H M S C L I C L A T S K K P N F
O D N C A A E I A N A I D N I A A J E N
H P E U M D N X R R L N A O S D T O W A
A P C T P A H E I N I O V M S H O R J X
L Y T N S K A T U C F I E F I T S E E H
K E I E H S P R R J O S N X M U E G R Q
O D C K I A V F L O R I D A H O N O S U
K V U E R L I E A I N A V L Y S N N E P
V Z T R E A W A S H I N G T O N I U Y K
A L A B A M A R Y L A N D T N O M R E V
```

ALABAMA	INDIANA	NEBRASKA	RHODE ISLAND
ALASKA	IOWA	NEVADA	SOUTH CAROLINA
ARIZONA	KANSAS	NEW HAMPSHIRE	SOUTH DAKOTA
ARKANSAS	KENTUCKY	NEW JERSEY	TENNESSEE
CALIFORNIA	LOUISIANA	NEW MEXICO	TEXAS
COLORADO	MARYLAND	NEW YORK	UTAH
CONNECTICUT	MASSACHUSETTS	NORTH CAROLINA	VERMONT
DELAWARE	MICHIGAN	NORTH DAKOTA	WASHINGTON
FLORIDA	MINNESOTA	OHIO	WEST VIRGINIA
HAWAII	MISSISSIPPI	OKLAHOMA	
IDAHO	MISSOURI	OREGON	
ILLINOIS	MONTANA	PENNSYLVANIA	

Solution on page 150

At the Movies

```
O N I C A P L A Y D N A C N H O J C M M
C E S O L C N N E L G H C X Y D G Y W E
A N P U A X A M Y I R V I N G C A U W G
J I R E L D I M E T T E B N H W R L K R
A L M O E A N W E T S E W E A M Y B A Y
M S E A T R N O S B I R R N J V B R N A
E H P R N P T A F W L Z U C O I U Y N N
S E A E O D I S T R E D Y B A V S N E P
D D L D T O Y R L U E R M J N I E N B P
E Y B B N E M G B Y R T D G C E Y E A E
A L G U A O R I A E R N E N R N L R X D
N A E T A G F F M R T E E P A L N L T Y
A M N T A E K Y A E C T M R W E K X E N
M A E O V K C R R L D I Y R F I I C R N
Y R A N T O M H A N K S A G O G H L Y H
W R U S H C L E W L E U Q A R H P J U O
E X T N A R G Y R A C H M Y D A A D Q J
N X R A M O P R A H F M E L G I B S O N
A S Y E J R Y C L I Z A M I N E L L I Q
J J A M E S C A A N N Y L F L O R R E Y
```

AL PACINO	FAYE DUNAWAY	JOHNNY DEPP	RED BUTTONS
AMY IRVING	GARY BUSEY	JULIE ANDREWS	RIP TORN
ANDY GARCIA	GENE AUTRY	LANA TURNER	TOM HANKS
ANNE BAXTER	GLENN CLOSE	LIZA MINELLI	VIVIEN LEIGH
BETTE MIDLER	HARPO MARX	MAE WEST	YUL BRYNNER
BETTY GRABLE	HEDY LAMARR	MEG RYAN	
CARY GRANT	HENRY FONDA	MEL GIBSON	
CHER	JAMES CAAN	MERYL STREEP	
CLARK GABLE	JAMES DEAN	PETER FALK	
DEMI MOORE	JANE WYMAN	PETER FONDA	
ELLEN BURSTYN	JOAN CRAWFORD	RAQUEL WELCH	
ERROL FLYNN	JOHN CANDY		

Solution on page 150

Land Creatures

```
L H G J W E S U O M J T Q L Q V S M M M
N H P N Y X L O T D C E N I P U C R O P
X L E P E D I G R E E I A E M E P D N K
P L P V N F C A C E S Q L A L O P B G Z
W U P K E Q P T K K C I T D R I T F O X
P R A C C O O N U U B O O A O D T I O P
C H F U E R G N C R P E N P N L V P S S
S I Y L R D K I E O K M C I R D P A E V
E O C A T T C G P A C H O P H O Y H R R
D Q P Q I N H P N A R K Z K W R P U I K
I E N G A A I S D E E A A G E C K O G N
A Y E X O H N Y B A T N B T L H T D T U
U R Y R J P C F A P S T I B I E W A L M
J A Y A T E H B D R M W I U I E A G I P
J A M T C L I L G X A E Z K G T L R H I
D C G A Z E L L E O H M L I Z A R D N H
T W M U L T L K R Y D A N E Y H U G E C
X E R N A L A E N C Z X B I D G S R B L
L A O I F R B O Z P U R N R U V J U X H
M D L H D B P M G A A X H Q G L B N Z J
```

AARDVARK	FOX	LIZARD	RACCOON
BADGER	GAZELLE	LLAMA	RAT
CAMEL	GECKO	MONGOOSE	REPTILE
CAT	GERBIL	MOUSE	RHINOCEROS
CHEETAH	GOAT	PARROT	SKUNK
CHINCHILLA	GUINEA PIG	PEDIGREE	SNAKE
CHIPMUNK	HAMSTER	PIG	TIGER
COCKATIEL	HIPPOPOTAMUS	PONY	WALRUS
DEER	HYENA	PORCUPINE	ZEBRA
DOG	JAGUAR	PORPOISE	
DOLPHIN	KITTEN	PUPPY	
ELEPHANT	LEOPARD	RABBIT	

Solution on page 151

Water Creatures

```
S T A R F I S H R S H A R K B R T A B P
G U P P Y O Y U S U S N A P P E R S E D
X B K G J A B Y D I I B H R L I A P L H
Y I M T U O O S E N F J H A Z L T P T L
T L B L U E G I L L Y D H C M L U R R E
M A R L I N C P T Q L W L O G E O B U S
Y H P E R C H O O U L O N O E G R U T S
H L A G T Z U D R C E R W M G N T W E U
B H D N C R B K R M J M E T R A O A O M
K G O O U C B A R R A C U D A N L G E Q
R X D P L T P O L L A C S L N I T U Y Z
J G W S F P A P S S B P K I L U L V A N
O Z R R I U H B C A Z C M E E L O S B Y
A Y H E G F F I S R O A P I R H A L A A
R C K T I F L S N D A M A L C E H L F C
S I B S Y E E U D I O B Z N C Z L O I R
P D U B J R X A K N M C A T F I S H W N
D S T O U K H E Y E L L A W Z V N C V N
T C B L H J H I N R C M N Q B H U O S W
K N F Y S Z X S C L N Z S V K F S G D U
```

ANCHOVY	DOLPHIN	MINNOW	SPONGE
ANGEL	FLOUNDER	MUSSEL	STARFISH
BARRACUDA	FLUKE	PERCH	STURGEON
BASS	GOBY	PIKE	TROUT
BLUEGILL	GOLDFISH	PUFFER	TUNA
CARP	GUPPY	SALMON	TURTLE
CATFISH	HADDOCK	SARDINE	WALLEYE
CHUB	HALIBUT	SCALLOP	WHALE
CLAM	JELLYFISH	SEAL	YELLOWTAIL
COD	LOBSTER	SHARK	
CRAB	MACKEREL	SNAPPER	
CRAPPIE	MARLIN	SOLE	

Solution on page 151

Money

```
T S H A I P U R U B E S I X P O Y S Q O
D G K R G U S Y K O X O X E A H C A W K
Y S S R U M B F S L Z J S R A N I D G P
K C K X A P R N F I I E L S A T O B Q N
C F L H R M E E H V T L R R I Y A L S N
R L R Q S S E E T A Y I F I L Y T A E A
E I S R B B U H S R R S J A L H Y W P G
D X N C U S S M C E Y S I Q Z V S Q O V
G B I G J J F G N S W M W A A H U J U V
U E K F G L U O N D T J I Y E N A M N B
Q R T T N I R O F I M U K K E R V C D X
W M Y W L K T G D J L D E N O I E F S H
I M L D B H N S G O Q L A D S A L O B P
S A E L A Z F V U Y S K I E M S D F S F
H R T B F A W P A Y L J U H O U V B A A
S K A E H U N S N S H R C H C Y T O L Z
P K B L X H O U H O O A J S K S K H Y F
H A X A L W R A N D R S E L B U R Q W N
Z A N B M O U B E D S Z E Y U V F W P X
A R P J K Q D Y R U E E I P H W A F Q I
```

BAHT
BOLIVARES
DEUTSCHE MARKS
DINARS
DIRHAMS
DOLLARS
DRACHMAE
ESCUDOS
EURO
FORINT
FRANCS
GUILDERS

KORUNY
KRONER
KWACHA
LEI
LEVA
LIRE
MARKKAA
NEW SHEKELS
PESETAS
PESOS
POUNDS
RAND

REAIS
RINGGITS
RIYALS
RUBLES
RUPEES
RUPIAHS
SCHILLINGS
YEN
ZLOTYCH

Solution on page 151

Naming Names

```
P X D F U Z H S B R D W U P Y X B R L E
U M S Z V P A I G E E E B R O O K E Y L
C B J N W M T N T F Z R N A D I A T Q B
G H Z J U Z A S U I V D L D D H L N M M
F A Z E E T K N B N S N I T C D Y U R B
I B L J R B G G N Y A V I C M S H C A
V E V E I N A H P E T S M O J M S A N S
V M L J X S B C P J L B N A X K A L E Z
X A E Q K A T H E R I N E E N N N L M A
C T W N S V N H H A O N L N R T I E M C
U T H O M A S D B R X I M C J J H B A H
J Z N N M N Z I R M Z C P Z A A X A Q A
T S C A Y N G Q K A D H V H W Z M S J R
H A G T F A I C B D G O C D E S T I N Y
M T Y A I H H E N I V L Y Z H T L X N J
A F N L R L T A N S Z A G B T Q K E U E
Z N H I O H D X N O O S R U T C L L N B
A F O E Y R P U U N K H A I A S I A E K
C C J H O D K A Y L A O C J M A Y E H D
N G X J I K T S A R A H E F C R W Q F O
```

ABIGAIL	CONNOR	JOHN	RYAN
AIDAN	DESTINY	JORDAN	SAMANTHA
ALEXANDRA	ELIJAH	JULIA	SAMUEL
ALEXIS	ELIZABETH	KATHERINE	SARAH
ALYSSA	EMMA	KAYLA	SAVANNAH
ANDREW	GRACE	MADISON	STEPHANIE
ANGEL	HANNAH	MATTHEW	TAYLOR
ANNA	HUNTER	MICHAEL	THOMAS
BENJAMIN	ISABELLA	NATALIE	ZACHARY
BROOKE	ISAIAH	NICHOLAS	
CALEB	JACK	NOAH	
CHLOE	JENNIFER	PAIGE	

Solution on page 151

U.S. Presidents

```
L Q E Z Z L R G Y R S N O S V C R G X K
V J S R B P Z Y D G C N G W S N N P G I
H J O V O L T E K L O P O A N V E G R I
U Z R Y C O O L I D G E A S R O L Y A T
D V Q B K L U N E Y M W M H R F S H N V
N H K M E N T I R V T H K I N E I L T A
C S S Y N O J K O E E A K N A H F E I R
D U M O N S N C M J I S F G G A A F L W
E B U A E K I M L A O S O T A R P Y E D
N M Y J D C X J L H D H E O E R T K E J
N Q Z Q Y A O I I N V I N N R I F C T S
D T R C D J N C F E A A S S H S M L F I
R E V T D C K E C O A M N O O O U E D H
G F H O O V E R X A R R U B N N W V T A
K T J L Y R E L Y T R D T R U Q A E W R
C Q N N I I Y U F Z P T O K T R W L R D
S H D U P O Q Z S L J E H D G O E A M I
Q R B H W Z A U Y Q T G B U C H A N A N
R X T U L V V T C A U R E T R A C D Q G
V J Y S U W L F L W X I N O X B T P A W
```

ADAMS	GARFIELD	MADISON	TYLER
ARTHUR	GRANT	MCKINLEY	VAN BUREN
BUCHANAN	HARDING	MONROE	WASHINGTON
BUSH	HARRISON	NIXON	WILSON
CARTER	HAYES	PIERCE	
CLEVELAND	HOOVER	POLK	
CLINTON	JACKSON	REAGAN	
COOLIDGE	JEFFERSON	ROOSEVELT	
EISENHOWER	JOHNSON	TAFT	
FILLMORE	KENNEDY	TAYLOR	
FORD	LINCOLN	TRUMAN	

Solution on page 151

The Periodic Table

```
C  L  T  N  O  D  A  R  A  D  I  U  M  C  O  P  P  E  R  I
A  U  M  U  I  B  R  E  T  T  Y  X  M  U  I  L  U  H  T  Z
R  M  R  Z  N  S  U  R  O  H  P  S  O  H  P  N  O  R  O  B
B  U  N  I  U  G  B  M  E  M  R  U  P  E  F  D  S  Z  Y  H
O  I  W  E  U  O  A  G  M  R  O  C  I  R  I  D  I  U  M  I
N  B  S  A  P  M  R  U  D  U  M  H  N  U  O  R  M  D  M  A
N  O  B  M  M  T  I  V  R  B  E  L  M  E  C  S  U  U  V  W
O  I  M  R  U  C  U  V  L  I  T  O  X  O  O  D  I  L  G  B
B  N  A  U  N  T  M  N  T  D  H  R  N  D  Y  N  S  U  J  H
E  W  C  A  I  O  H  H  I  I  I  I  Q  G  R  I  E  T  M  P
L  N  R  F  M  D  A  S  N  U  U  N  Y  O  U  Q  N  E  U  B
I  F  I  P  U  L  A  I  B  M  M  E  F  Q  C  S  G  T  N  F
U  P  W  T  L  L  C  L  U  S  H  I  Q  T  R  A  A  I  E  J
M  Q  C  I  A  K  J  I  L  C  L  G  I  O  E  M  M  U  D  U
U  U  U  M  E  T  N  A  G  A  L  L  I  U  M  A  P  M  B  M
I  M  I  L  H  O  S  K  C  N  P  J  M  U  I  R  T  T  Y  S
D  V  Q  S  L  C  J  A  D  D  V  C  A  L  C  I  U  M  L  C
N  P  R  O  S  D  B  M  U  I  N  F  A  H  M  U  I  D  O  S
I  K  P  K  H  A  I  O  F  U  P  C  H  R  O  M  I  U  M  E
L  L  A  G  S  W  H  X  I  M  U  I  N  E  L  E  S  H  B  S
```

ALUMINUM	DYSPROSIUM	NEPTUNIUM	SAMARIUM
ASTATINE	FRANCIUM	NICKEL	SCANDIUM
BARIUM	GALLIUM	NIOBIUM	SELENIUM
BISMUTH	HAFNIUM	NOBELIUM	SODIUM
BORON	HASSIUM	PALLADIUM	THALLIUM
CALCIUM	INDIUM	PHOSPHORUS	THULIUM
CALIFORNIUM	IRIDIUM	POLONIUM	YTTERBIUM
CARBON	LUTETIUM	PROMETHIUM	YTTRIUM
CHLORINE	MAGNESIUM	RADIUM	ZIRCONIUM
CHROMIUM	MERCURY	RADON	
COPPER	MOLYBDENUM	RHODIUM	
CURIUM	NEON	RUBIDIUM	

Solution on page 151

Athletes

```
L M A G I C J O H N S O N M L N A Y D R
J O H N N Y U N I T A S C A O H B K A E
S M A I L L I W D E T F R T N M A R E V
X S D N O B Y R R A B R Y O X R K E N A
I N G N N H Q T D G Y A S R E H E N S L
F N N A I N L W A B P N V E A R H G M D
U A I M H R W C I R I T M K R E M A A O
Z M W N I A L R E B M A H C T L I W S R
Z S E O H M D T O E B R K E H L C S R S
Y I K T J O L R S D I K R B U I H U E U
Z E C Y S A E O U S A E U S R M A N D A
O H I E W I R L S N V N Q I A E E O N L
E T R P K E J A A A J T V R S I L H A K
L E T C T A G G E Y R O J O H G J N S C
L O A E B A O S C M V N N B E G O U N I
E J P B E H M O A L L E N I V E R S O N
R Y A R N O L D P A L M E R D R D U I K
P R D E T T E R R Y B R A D S H A W E C
N N B R G Y J U L I U S E R V I N G D A
A S A M O H T H A I S I B I X O E D K J
```

ALLEN IVERSON	JACK NICKLAUS	REGGIE MILLER
ANDRE AGASSI	JACKIE ROBINSON	ROD LAVER
ARNOLD PALMER	JOE THEISMANN	SAM SNEAD
ARTHUR ASHE	JOHNNY UNITAS	TED WILLIAMS
BARRY BONDS	JULIUS ERVING	TERRY BRADSHAW
BEN HOGAN	KAREEM ABDUL JABBAR	TOM SEAVER
BORIS BECKER	LARRY BIRD	WALTER PAYTON
DEION SANDERS	MAGIC JOHNSON	WILT CHAMBERLAIN
FRAN TARKENTON	MICHAEL JORDAN	
FUZZY ZOELLER	PATRICK EWING	
HONUS WAGNER	PETE ROSE	
ISIAH THOMAS	PEYTON MANNING	

Solution on page 152

How's the Weather

```
D J L E W O P D T Z S J X P H W K R W B
E I G O P H L Q Q H W W R M P X N W L G
E B V O K O S Z X N I A R D I C A S W F
L W C E C Y H Y Y D U O L C T G G I O A
X L I W O Q R U P T T X T S O R F G B K
I W A N S E W O N S G N I W O L B J N L
U N Y F D F K C T B S G N I N T H G I L
E O N N N Y X S S N O W F A L L J J A S
J O U O I I U J R L T M C Q N C M T R Z
H H Z U W D A A O E R R B O I W E O T Q
T P X K T V E R E O B P M Q A J N R U N
A Y I A E L O L W E A T H E R V A N E O
R T A I C E S T O R M J V R G N C A N D
T W E A T H E R B A L L O O N L I D O R
T P R E C I P I T A T I O N I K R O L I
T F M G B J D V T O U E Z M Z W R B C Z
B X J A L L T Q H S S K A S E L U Z Y Z
V A D D O O N D W K I T Y D E I H P C L
G F R Y J P R J M T E M P E R A T U R E
H W F U T B A V V S D O O L F H X U Z B
```

ACID RAIN	FREEZING RAIN	SNOWFALL
BLOWING SNOW	FROST	TEMPERATURE
CLEAR	HAIL	THUNDER
CLIMATE	HURRICANE	TORNADO
CLOUDY	ICE STORM	TYPHOON
COLD	LIGHTNING	WEATHER BALLOON
CYCLONE	METEOROLOGIST	WEATHER VANE
DEW	MIST	WINDSOCK
DRIZZLE	PRECIPITATION	WINDY
DUST STORM	RAINBOW	
FLOOD	RAINFALL	
FOG	SLEET	

Solution on page 152

Fruits and Vegetables

```
C K M U B Y Z P A P A Y A R K O B C E H
M P E B O R R A A Y E N M P H K H D V I
Q G L E Z F G R E E N P E P P E R A W Z
L N O M M I S R E P U O L A T N A C T Q
F Z N I N N E N Y B L B P C O C O N U T
L N Z L I I I K R R N S I L O C C O R B
K G W P P R K E O L R E L P P A J L N L
O U Y A E E B P A H G E S V S D G E I O
X A M G T M A L M H C I B Y S N R M P M
A V N K U E E C A U L I F L O W E R M P
B A Y C S T R P H C P Q T V U B E E W Z
T B U R T L R C V K K O U R Y M N T C B
A C P U R I I C R L B B T H A R B A X A
U W C J C E H T E E B N E A C N E W U D
Q E R O N U B S N B S D O R T A A L X J
M Y T F L Q Q N B E G S I I R O N N E M
U X A I M U L P A R L E M O N Y S I A C
K M T A A N E Y R R E B N A G O L Y P B
K R A S P B E R R Y C A R R O T U G Z S
F U H V H Y X T I F V X L Y M D Z P P N
```

APPLE	COCONUT	LIME	PUMPKIN
APRICOT	CRANBERRY	LOGANBERRY	RASPBERRY
ARTICHOKE	CUCUMBER	MELON	SPINACH
BANANA	FIG	MULBERRY	SQUASH
BEET	GREEN BEANS	OKRA	TANGERINE
BLACKBERRY	GREEN PEPPER	ONION	TURNIP
BOYSENBERRY	GUAVA	PAPAYA	WATERCRESS
BROCCOLI	HUCKLEBERRY	PARSNIP	WATERMELON
CANTALOUPE	KUMQUAT	PEACH	YAM
CARROT	LEMON	PERSIMMON	
CAULIFLOWER	LENTILS	PLUM	
CELERY	LETTUCE	POTATO	

Solution on page 152

Grammatical

```
K D U V D O I R E P R O N O U N K S V N
Z O S E S E H T N E R A P G O R G E R E
I E H P O R T S O P A A N L A N R N P J
Y G N I L L E P S W R I O M I B P T H E
E G C T A W E N C T N C N M A V C E R S
K X I A R S X I I I I O M F I C A N A N
O D N L U W K C L M I A R N O N P C S E
M M F I L S I R E T R A T N F O I E E T
I N I C P P E S A G G E J B D I T V N C
V A N S L D U M A M R U T N R T A I C E
P Y I E N A A I E J N M F E W I L S O J
G R T U L L D N E C W O R D D S I S M B
Y A I C C B T C T L E X I C O N Z E P U
Z L V X A R T I C L E T R T N A A S O S
Q U E S T I O N M A R K N U A R T S U V
C B S R O N O X P R E P O S I T I O N T
J A D N O I T A U T C N U P D K O P D Z
S C O M M A B B R E V I A T I O N U U X
M O D I F I E R V P M P N E H P Y H Q R
E V I T C E J D A D V E R B N H V U H Q
```

ABBREVIATION	EXCLAMATION MARK	PHRASE	TENSE
ADJECTIVE	FRAGMENT	PLURAL	TRANSITION
ADVERB	HYPHEN	POSSESSIVE	UNDERLINING
APOSTROPHE	INFINITIVES	PREPOSITION	VERB
ARTICLE	INTERJECTION	PRONOUN	VOCABULARY
CAPITALIZATION	ITALICS	PUNCTUATION	WORD
CLAUSE	LEXICON	QUESTION MARK	
COMMA	MODIFIER	QUOTATION MARKS	
COMPOUND	NOUN	SEMICOLON	
CONJUNCTION	PARENTHESES	SENTENCE	
DETERMINERS	PARTICIPLE	SPELLING	
DIAGRAMMING	PERIOD	SUBJECT	

Solution on page 152

U.S. National Parks

```
B S D N A L D A B R Y C E C A N Y O N A
C A N Y O N L A N D S R H C D E N A L I
J O M E S A V E R D E A U N Y C K G C O
H C L V L V S K R I N Y D N E B G I B U
F O Z R D A D O N N A F L I A M T A K Q
R N S X G W J I E H X W I N D C A V E E
T G E U E F A L O D R Y T O R T U G A S
N A A X I R I G C N O Y N A C D N A R G
G R E A T S A N D D U N E S E H C R A R
O E N N L V X D E A T H V A L L E Y W A
R E U A A M A M M O T H C A V E Z I O N
K O N L T S E R O F D E I F I R T E P D
M D L F E E R L O T I P A C A D I A Z T
S E F C A R L S B A D C A V E R N S M E
Y H X N N Y E L L A V K U B O K F D P T
C R C R A T E R L A K E N Y A C S I B O
N O Y N A C S G N I K R A L C E K A L N
P L T G L A C I E R B A Y O S E M I T E
W N I S A B T A E R G H A L E A K A L A
G A H O T S P R I N G S R U E G A Y O V
```

ACADIA
ARCHES
BADLANDS
BIG BEND
BISCAYNE
BRYCE CANYON
CANYONLANDS
CAPITOL REEF
CARLSBAD CAVERNS
CHANNEL ISLANDS
CONGAREE
CRATER LAKE

CUYAHOGA VALLEY
DEATH VALLEY
DENALI
DRY TORTUGAS
GATES OF THE ARCTIC
GLACIER BAY
GRAND CANYON
GRAND TETON
GREAT BASIN
GREAT SAND DUNES
HALEAKALA
HOT SPRINGS

KATMAI
KENAI FJORDS
KINGS CANYON
KOBUK VALLEY
LAKE CLARK
MAMMOTH CAVE
MESA VERDE
MOUNT RAINIER
PETRIFIED FOREST
SAGUARO
SEQUOIA
VOYAGEURS

WIND CAVE
YOSEMITE
ZION

Solution on page 152

```
C Y P F L T W S R E V I R R G Q F X H T
T E N N I S G T L Q B B L U P N B G U T
V L D A N J P N J U G B L L H J I N S U
D G E O T G W O N E A K A V I A T I O N
P H S J M U N Q B S C Y B H M F C E K W
U E S S O F R I K T G N E I L L Y O L S
U I E L U F V E K R P Z S K I O X N S J
U X N D N L T C O I B H A M D G J A L E
N K R A T B G U U A H X B B G H N C I D
Y N E C A X N E C N G I M G N I L I A S
G C D L I D I K A G N I D R I B L N R N
O N L S N D P L U G I P V J H J D C T O
K J I K S A M H D G K W R N S Z C I R W
V S W K C Q A Z U W I D E A I E S P A I
E V O K A F C R B N B E A R F A Q E E X
V W X B Y Y G E B M T A C Q S T R O P S
H B S J B O A T I N G I W A L K I N G A
F Z A B U C S K A G N I N N U R R N M Z
T Y G L H C Y C L I N G H G G L O R G R
P D U M L Z F O P L E I Z C C A W Y V S
```

AVIATION	CLIMBING	PLAYGROUND	WILDERNESS
BACKPACK	CYCLING	RAFTING	
BALL	EQUESTRIAN	RIVERS	
BASEBALL	FISHING	RUNNING	
BASKETBALL	GOLF	SAILING	
BEACH	HIKING	SCUBA	
BIKING	HUNTING	SKIING	
BIRDING	KAYAKING	SNOW	
BOATING	MOUNTAINS	SPORTS	
CAMPING	NATURE	TENNIS	
CANOEING	OCEAN	TRAILS	
CANTEEN	PICNIC	WALKING	

Solution on page 152

Musical People

```
S H O S T A K O V I C H O P I N D C M A
M A C S S M W Y N T O N M A R S A L I S
U S O S C A R L A T T I L E E N V N C G
T D U R H A J E S O E A K Z T Y E O A N
A A N E U Q R L V K N R B M R L B T R U
T V T C B O O H R J A O R I O E R P O O
T E B R E H I A A P H T A E P K U M L Y
R S A E R W L Y E M Z T H H E A B A E R
A T S M T C L I B S M E M D L L E H K E
E A I Y Y E L E I C R E S N O B C L I T
R M E N R R R L D B T U R O C T K E N S
O P N N A L O U I S A R M S T R O N G E
C E E H I B E E T H O V E N T A U O I L
K R C O W A H S E I T R A E T E S I N C
C N Z J B A R R Y G I B B H Z M I L I B
I R V I N G B E R L I N V P E E Q N C A
H P R C D I Z Z Y G I L L E S P I E C R
C B O A N A M E L O C E T T E N R O U B
Y C W X T H E L O N I O U S M O N K P E
K N H O S S L E D N E M B R U C K N E R
```

ALAN JAY LERNER	CHICK COREA	LESTER YOUNG	THELONIOUS MONK
ART BLAKELY	CHOPIN	LIONEL HAMPTON	WYNTON MARSALIS
ART TATUM	COLE PORTER	LISZT	
ARTIE SHAW	COUNT BASIE	LOUIS ARMSTRONG	
BARBER	DAVE BRUBECK	MENDELSSOHN	
BARRY GIBB	DAVE STAMPER	ORNETTE COLEMAN	
BEETHOVEN	DIZZY GILLESPIE	OSCAR HAMMERSTEIN	
BERLIOZ	HERBIE HANCOCK	PUCCINI	
BRAHMS	HOLST	SCARLATTI	
BRUCKNER	IRVING BERLIN	SCHUBERT	
CAROLE KING	JOHNNY MERCER	SHOSTAKOVICH	
CHARLIE PARKER	KENNY CLARKE	STEPHEN SONDHEIM	

Solution on page 153

Sports

```
C Q L L L A B Y E L L O V W N W O J G U
F U G L A G J A T H L E T I C S S U Y F
H O R N A O E S S O R C A L O T L D M O
T T O L I B O J U K B A D M I N T O N R
S E S T I C E X D F E N C I N G T C A Q
K N K U B N A S M A R T I A L A R T S I
A N I C X A G R A J A W B N E O A L T D
T I I E I I L O E B M Z P A S V C Z I V
I S N F R R U L L S D S L S L D K E C K
N G G E B T C E T F R Y C V M L J S S I
G W N U D S T M A U T O R A C I N G C A
N S D O R E C C O S U P H S A U Q S Y E
I Y O A N U H Y G N I L T S E R W G C F
H R R N M Q R F T R I A T H L O N N L R
S J I C H E E R L E A D I N G I A I I W
I S K C H S Y E K C O H Z L T D F N N A
F V M C J V G N I L W O B O A T I N G H
D A R T S T O Z G N I X O B Y B G U R A
S A I L I N G D C M P H G N I W O R S J
F P S L L A B T F O S W I M M I N G N R
```

ARCHERY	CURLING	JUDO	SOFTBALL
ATHLETICS	CYCLING	LACROSSE	SQUASH
AUTO RACING	DANCE	MARTIAL ARTS	SWIMMING
BADMINTON	DARTS	OUTDOORS	TABLE TENNIS
BASEBALL	EQUESTRIAN	ROWING	TENNIS
BASKETBALL	FENCING	RUGBY	TRACK
BOATING	FISHING	RUNNING	TRIATHLON
BOWLING	FOOTBALL	SAILING	VOLLEYBALL
BOXING	GOLF	SHOOTING	WRESTLING
CHEERLEADING	GYMNASTICS	SKATING	
CRICKET	HOCKEY	SKIING	
CROSS COUNTRY	HORSE RACING	SOCCER	

Solution on page 153

5

Mazes

These mazes will sharpen your visual-spatial intelligence. All shapes and sizes of mazes await you here. Some of them can be solved quickly, while others will demand more concentration. Every maze has just one answer. Here is a simple tip: when you come to a dead end, retrace your way back to where a path choice was made and take the alternative route. Using this technique, you can make your way through any of these mazes.

Rectangle 1

Solution on page 153

Rectangle 2

Solution on page 153

Rectangle 3

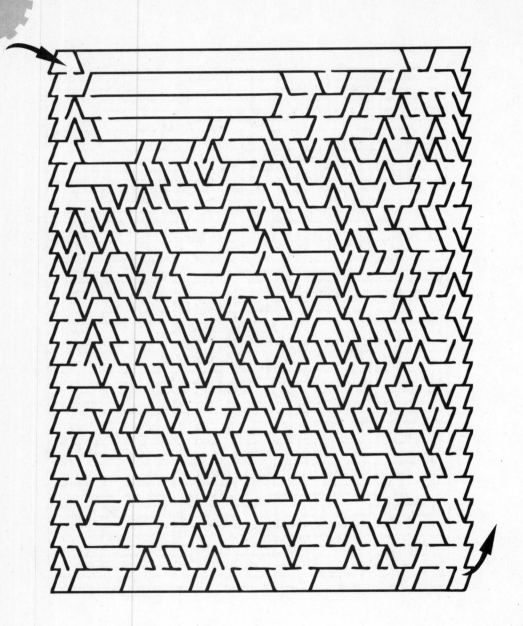

Solution on page 153

Concentric 1

Solution on page 154

Concentric 2

Solution on page 154

Concentric 3

Solution on page 154

Break In

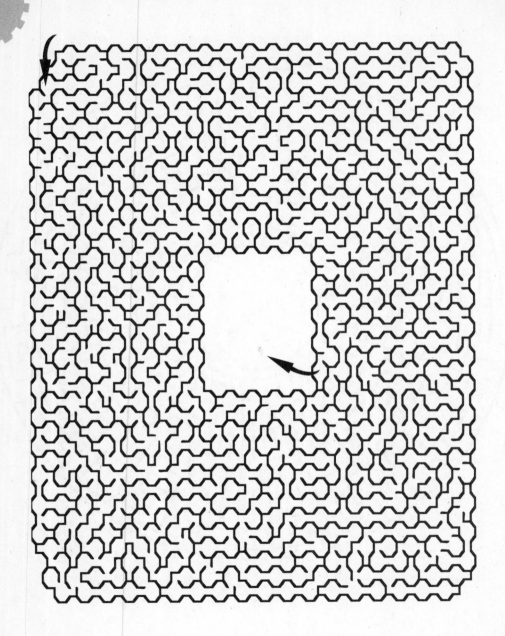

Solution on page 154

Break Out

Solution on page 154

Circle

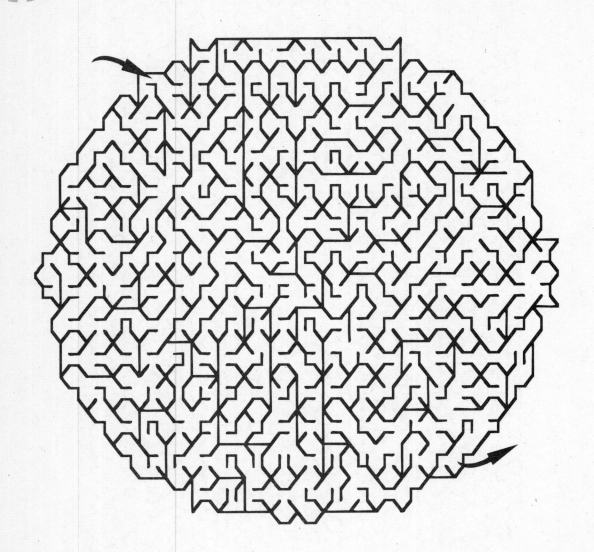

Solution on page 154

Oval

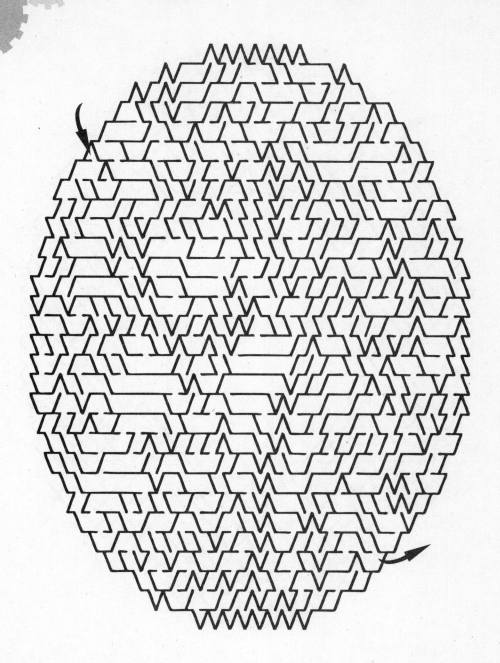

Solution on page 155

Wheel

Solution on page 155

Triangle

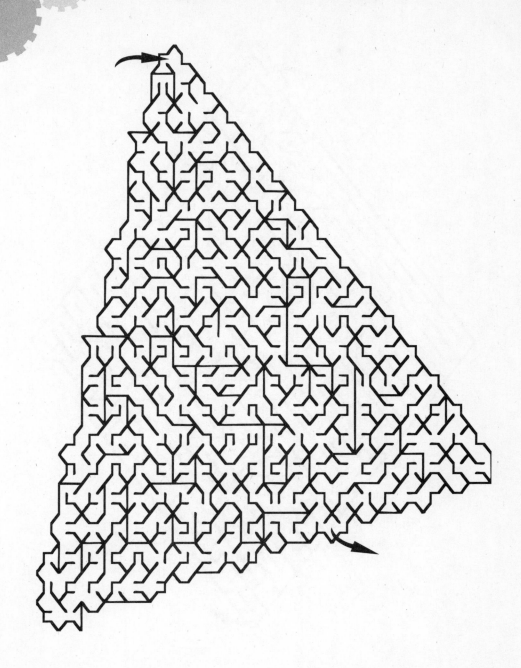

Solution on page 155

Diamond

Solution on page 155

Hexagon

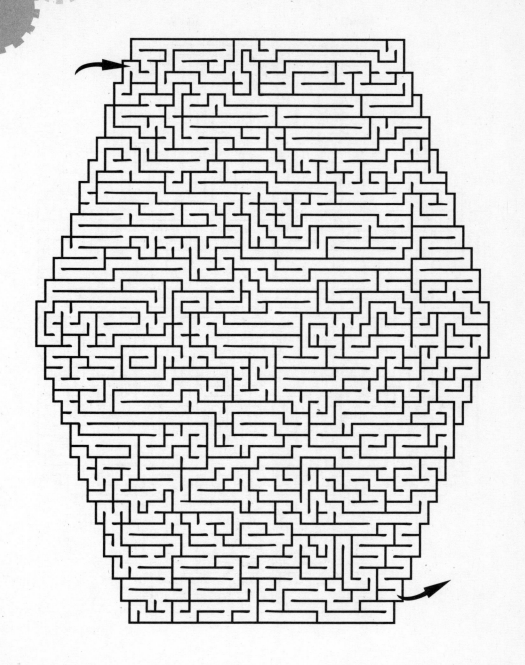

Solution on page 155

Octagon

Solution on page 155

Pentagon

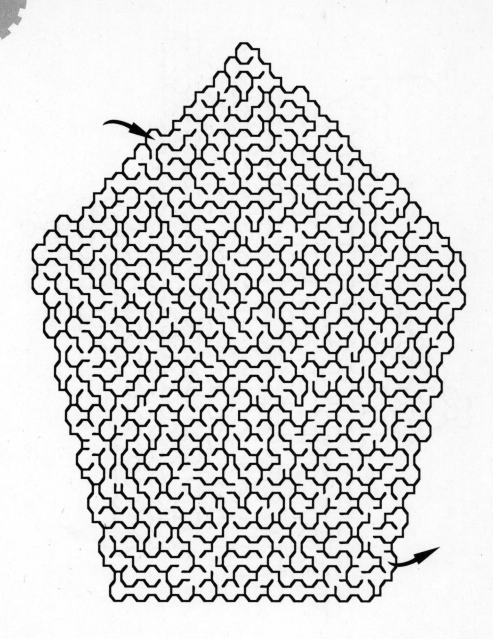

Solution on page 156

Star

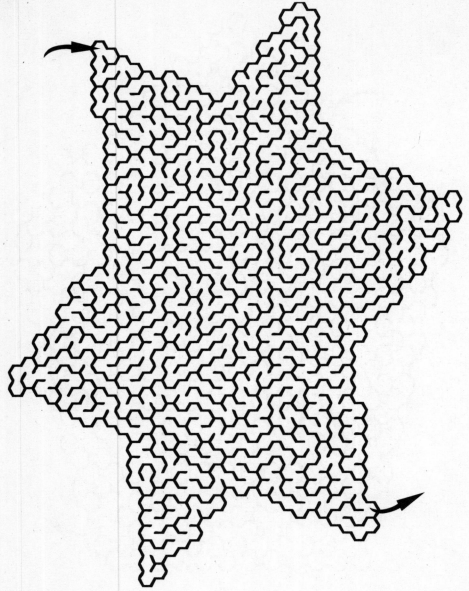

Solution on page 156

6

Scrambled Categories

Unscramble the letters to form words. All of the words in each group belong in the given category. You will be able to unscramble many of these immediately, while others will take more thought.

Parts of a Book

1. INSEP   _____

2. GPSEA   _____

3. OVCRE   _____

5. BGIDINN   _____

Musical

1. TUEMRPT   _____

2. GIUART   _____

3. AIPNO   _____

4. DUMR   _____

5. ILNVIO   _____

Bake a Cake

1. URFOL   _____

2. SGUAR   _____

3. GGSE   _____

4. UTRBTE   _____

5. LMIK   _____

Solutions on page 156

Colorful

1. UPPLRE   _____

2. OLLWEY   _____

3. GENRE   _____

4. AOGREN   _____

5. ROBNW   _____

Things in the Kitchen

1. TLUPASA   _____

2. FKNIE   _____

3. ENVO   _____

4. EDNELRB   _____

5. REGREORIFRTA   _____

Things in the Workshop

1. VVERDREIRSC   _____

2. EMRAMH   _____

3. RNWECH   _____

4. DLILR   _____

5. RSLIEP   _____

Solutions on pages 156–157

What Does Your Garden Grow?

1. CNOR   _____

2. UHAQSS   _____

3. AEOMOTTS   _____

4. ROSTCRA   _____

5. EWTNMOLAER _____

- -

On the Water

1. ENCAO   _____

2. KAYKA   _____

3. ASIOATBL   _____

4. RTOATMOOB   _____

5. FART   _____

- -

The Shirt on Your Back

1. NTOUBT   _____

2. RLLACO   _____

3. ELSEEV   _____

4. TCEOKP   _____

5. FBIACR   _____

- -

Solutions on page 157

Auto Parts

1. RETIS   _____
2. NEEGIN   _____
3. ASRBKE   _____
4. REFULMF   _____
5. WDNLIHEIDS   _____

Legal Words

1. JDEGU   _____
2. AEYNTORT   _____
3. INWETSS   _____
4. UYJR   _____
5. RTUOC   _____

Electronic

1. IORDA   _____
2. ETILIENVSO   _____
3. ECTMORUP   _____
4. REVOMIWAC   _____
5. OREEST   _____

Solutions on page 157

Sports

1. BAELAKLTSB   _____

2. SLALEBAB   _____

3. LFOLOBTA   _____

4. KCHEYO   _____

5. COECSR   _____

Out of This World

1. ULPOT   _____

2. IEUTRPJ   _____

3. NESUV   _____

4. RTSUNA   _____

5. MYRECUR   _____

Halloween Costumes

1. CTHIW   _____

2. SHOGT   _____

3. IRESCNPS   _____

4. TMSRONE   _____

5. TAERIP   _____

Solutions on page 158

Drive Through

1. ERSETT   _____

2. NEVUAE   _____

3. REIVD   _____

4. WHAGYHI   _____

5. PWYAKAR   _____

- -

Make Haste

1. IKQUC   _____

2. EEPYSD   _____

3. PTMRPO   _____

4. PDRAI   _____

5. FIWST   _____

- -

Drawing Tools

1. HUTNBISPRA   _____

2. AEKMRR   _____

3. PNCELI   _____

4. YCORNA   _____

5. AKHLC   _____

- -

Solutions on page 158

Things in the Bathroom

1. ITELTO _____

2. TTBUBAH _____

3. INSK _____

4. RRMIRO _____

5. EWSOHR _____

Literary Genres

1. YSMTREY _____

2. CEMANRO _____

3. PRYTEO _____

4. VLEONS _____

5. ISASCSCL _____

Star Sign

1. NCPRCRIAO _____

2. OOSPIRC _____

3. AUIQSRUA _____

4. GSTRUTSAIIA _____

5. TSRUAU _____

Solutions on pages 158–159

Family Life

1. DANGARM   _____

2. TNAU   _____

3. ISNCUO   _____

4. NLUCE   _____

5. THREBRO   _____

Tree Parts

1. UTKNR   _____

2. ESAVLE   _____

3. ORTSO   _____

4. SAHERBCN   _____

5. KRAB   _____

Water

1. RSRORIEVE   _____

2. DNOP   _____

3. RVEIR   _____

4. RASTME   _____

5. RKCEE   _____

Solutions on page 159

Computer System

1. EMROYM   _____
2. ROOTMIN   _____
3. ITERPNR   _____
4. KYBAEDOR   _____
5. OUMES   _____

Land Features

1. NTMNIUAO   _____
2. LYVLAE   _____
3. NNAOYC   _____
4. NOLOVCA   _____
5. EULAPAT   _____

Wedding

1. IDRBE   _____
2. OGMOR   _____
3. NOYHNEOOM   _____
4. RIAAMGRE   _____
5. AGENEETNMG   _____

Solutions on page 159

Parts of a Bicycle

1. ANERBDAHL _____

2. CHINA _____

3. EPSLDA _____

4. SEBKAR _____

5. DSALDE _____

- -

Cheese Please

1. HDEADRC _____

2. GAUDO _____

3. ISSWS _____

4. ECANMRIA _____

5. LAMZEOLRAZ _____

- -

Home Sweet Home

1. EBADO _____

2. CIEESNEDR _____

3. EPANMRTTA _____

4. IWDLLGNE _____

5. MNMUONICDIO_____

- -

Solutions on pages 159–160

Bakery Treats

1. RAINSOSTC   _____

2. REDBA   _____

3. HUGONDTU   _____

4. NIUMFF   _____

5. NCSEO   _____

Chessmen

1. WPAN   _____

2. KOOR   _____

3. IKNTHG   _____

4. HIBSPO   _____

5. NUEQE   _____

Card Games

1. REOPK   _____

2. RIDBEG   _____

3. MUYRM   _____

4. ISOTLRAEI   _____

5. KCCBAAKIJ   _____

Solutions on page 160–161

Triplet Puzzles

Determine the common word that can be combined with each of the three given words. For example, consider these three words: *trap*, *prize*, and *out*. The common word is *door*, which makes the answers *trapdoor*, *door prize*, and *outdoor*. Compounds can be open (*high school*), closed (*schoolhouse*) or hyphenated (*school-age*).

Triplet 1

1. tooth
2. up
3. paint

_____

Triplet 2

1. butter
2. cake
3. suction

_____

Triplet 3

1. clip
2. back
3. news

_____

Triplet 4

1. ache
2. artichoke
3. worm

_____

Triplet 5

1. good
2. power
3. living

_____

Triplet 6

1. dance
2. button
3. pork

_____

Triplet 7

1. drift
2. chuck
3. red

_____

Triplet 8

1. cake
2. stop
3. wave

_____

Triplet 9

1. book
2. key
3. worthy

_____

Triplet 10

1. bulb
2. flash
3. moon

_____

Triplet 11

1. down
2. game
3. case

_____

Triplet 12

1. pit
2. gap
3. watch

_____

Solutions on pages 160–161

Triplet 13

1. black
2. cast
3. break

_____

Triplet 19

1. bottom
2. blue
3. dumb

_____

Triplet 14

1. fountain
2. pal
3. bull

_____

Triplet 20

1. easy
2. man
3. high

_____

Triplet 15

1. stem
2. phone
3. cancer

_____

Triplet 21

1. chair
2. big
3. cart

_____

Triplet 16

1. white
2. winner
3. stick

_____

Triplet 22

1. score
2. wheeler
3. eyes

_____

Triplet 17

1. bed
2. Christmas
3. keeper

_____

Triplet 23

1. dance
2. plan
3. ground

_____

Triplet 18

1. back
2. first
3. held

_____

Triplet 24

1. basket
2. point
3. corn

_____

Solutions on page161

Triplet 25

1. blow
2. roar _____
3. clean

Triplet 26

1. book
2. pay _____
3. mate

Triplet 27

1. black
2. room _____
3. surf

Triplet 28

1. brain
2. cloth _____
3. white

Triplet 29

1. bad
2. wash _____
3. loud

Triplet 30

1. moon
2. dew _____
3. bee

Triplet 31

1. coat
2. gate _____
3. cotton

Triplet 32

1. neck
2. spring _____
3. heart

Triplet 33

1. rain
2. kick _____
3. gum

Triplet 34

1. bull's
2. witness _____
3. ball

Triplet 35

1. paste
2. sweet _____
3. pick

Triplet 36

1. hot
2. wood _____
3. bull

Solutions on page 162

Triplet 37

1. cease
2. cracker
3. wild

_____

Triplet 38

1. bean
2. table
3. break

_____

Triplet 39

1. mark
2. locked
3. Ice

_____

Triplet 40

1. vault
2. fishing
3. north

_____

Triplet 41

1. flag
2. shape
3. space

_____

Triplet 42

1. trip
2. horse
3. grid

_____

Triplet 43

1. loader
2. care
3. hand

_____

Triplet 44

1. strangle
2. up
3. house

_____

Triplet 45

1. guard
2. busy
3. some

_____

Triplet 46

1. home
2. bench
3. patch

_____

Triplet 47

1. needle
2. view
3. pin

_____

Triplet 48

1. flash
2. board
3. post

_____

Solutions on pages 162–163

Triplet 49

1. stir
2. small _____
3. French

Triplet 50

1. happy
2. glass _____
3. rush

Triplet 51

1. dipper
2. chicken _____
3. league

Triplet 52

1. blood
2. main _____
3. line

Triplet 53

1. common
2. cuts _____
3. shoulder

Triplet 54

1. brass
2. worm _____
3. wedding

Triplet 55

1. boiler
2. glass _____
3. paper

Triplet 56

1. backer
2. clothes _____
3. border

Triplet 57

1. station
2. home _____
3. data

Triplet 58

1. home
2. turner _____
3. boy

Triplet 59

1. ground
2. pack _____
3. horse

Triplet 60

1. ladder
2. foot _____
3. mother

Solutions on page 163

Triplet 61

1. office
2. soap _____
3. mail

Triplet 62

1. combat
2. end _____
3. comfort

Triplet 63

1. ground
2. mate _____
3. word

Triplet 64

1. six
2. back _____
3. rat

Triplet 65

1. box
2. junk _____
3. black

Triplet 66

1. marker
2. keeper _____
3. year

Triplet 67

1. fish
2. super _____
3. dust

Triplet 68

1. scarlet
2. head _____
3. love

Triplet 69

1. laughing
2. Wood _____
3. broker

Triplet 70

1. coming
2. motor _____
3. maker

Triplet 71

1. bath
2. mate _____
3. class

Triplet 72

1. cover
2. saw _____
3. storm

Solutions on page 163–164

Triplet 73

1. saver
2. wild _____
3. style

Triplet 74

1. wolf
2. battle _____
3. baby

Triplet 75

1. count
2. melt _____
3. stairs

Triplet 76

1. bulb
2. news _____
3. back

Triplet 77

1. copy
2. finish _____
3. journalism

Triplet 78

1. melon
2. dish _____
3. proof

Triplet 79

1. lame
2. soup _____
3. sitting

Triplet 80

1. flower
2. scout _____
3. Friday

Triplet 81

1. lifter
2. barber _____
3. window

Triplet 82

1. parallel
2. way _____
3. trailer

Triplet 83

1. table
2. zone _____
3. bitter

Solutions on page 164

What's in a Name?

Find words using only the letters in a given name. Each letter in a name can be used only once in your word. For example, if the name is George Washington, then you could make the words soar, grow, note, and many others. Words that are always capitalized or require a hyphen or an apostrophe are not included in the answer lists. Words with variant or British spellings are also not included.

Chris Evert

Find 10 four-letter words:

1. _____
2. _____
3. _____
4. _____
5. _____
6. _____
7. _____
8. _____
9. _____
10. _____

Fred MacMurray

Find 10 four-letter words:

1. _____
2. _____
3. _____
4. _____
5. _____
6. _____
7. _____
8. _____
9. _____
10. _____

Jacques Cousteau

Find 10 four-letter words:

1. _____
2. _____
3. _____
4. _____
5. _____
6. _____
7. _____
8. _____
9. _____
10. _____

Richard Gere

Find 10 four-letter words:

1. _____
2. _____
3. _____
4. _____
5. _____
6. _____
7. _____
8. _____
9. _____
10. _____

Solutions on page 165

Ginger Rogers

Find 10 four-letter words:

1. _____
2. _____
3. _____
4. _____
5. _____
6. _____
7. _____
8. _____
9. _____
10. _____

Cat Stevens

Find 10 four-letter words:

1. _____
2. _____
3. _____
4. _____
5. _____
6. _____
7. _____
8. _____
9. _____
10. _____

J. Edgar Hoover

Find 10 four-letter words:

1. _____
2. _____
3. _____
4. _____
5. _____
6. _____
7. _____
8. _____
9. _____
10. _____

Sam Donaldson

Find 10 four-letter words:

1. _____
2. _____
3. _____
4. _____
5. _____
6. _____
7. _____
8. _____
9. _____
10. _____

Solutions on page 166

Jason Robards

Find 10 four-letter words:

1. _____
2. _____
3. _____
4. _____
5. _____
6. _____
7. _____
8. _____
9. _____
10. _____

Keanu Reeves

Find 10 four-letter words:

1. _____
2. _____
3. _____
4. _____
5. _____
6. _____
7. _____
8. _____
9. _____
10. _____

Farrah Fawcett

Find 10 four-letter words:

1. _____
2. _____
3. _____
4. _____
5. _____
6. _____
7. _____
8. _____
9. _____
10. _____

Conan O'Brien

Find 10 four-letter words:

1. _____
2. _____
3. _____
4. _____
5. _____
6. _____
7. _____
8. _____
9. _____
10. _____

Solutions on pages 166–167

James Baker

Find 10 four-letter words:

1. _____
2. _____
3. _____
4. _____
5. _____
6. _____
7. _____
8. _____
9. _____
10. _____

Federico Fellini

Find 7 five-letter words:

1. _____
2. _____
3. _____
4. _____
5. _____
6. _____
7. _____

Art Linkletter

Find 7 five-letter words:

1. _____
2. _____
3. _____
4. _____
5. _____
6. _____
7. _____

Alfred Nobel

Find 7 five-letter words:

1. _____
2. _____
3. _____
4. _____
5. _____
6. _____
7. _____

Solutions on pages 167–168

Goldie Hawn

Find 7 five-letter words:

1. _____
2. _____
3. _____
4. _____
5. _____
6. _____
7. _____

Dianne Feinstein

Find 7 five-letter words:

1. _____
2. _____
3. _____
4. _____
5. _____
6. _____
7. _____

Amelia Earhart

Find 7 five-letter words:

1. _____
2. _____
3. _____
4. _____
5. _____
6. _____
7. _____

Milton Berle

Find 7 five-letter words:

1. _____
2. _____
3. _____
4. _____
5. _____
6. _____
7. _____

Solutions on pages 168–169

Margaret Thatcher

Find 7 five-letter words:

1. _____
2. _____
3. _____
4. _____
5. _____
6. _____
7. _____

Gerard Depardieu

Find 7 five-letter words:

1. _____
2. _____
3. _____
4. _____
5. _____
6. _____
7. _____

Regis Philbin

Find 7 five-letter words:

1. _____
2. _____
3. _____
4. _____
5. _____
6. _____
7. _____

Barry Manilow

Find 7 five-letter words:

1. _____
2. _____
3. _____
4. _____
5. _____
6. _____
7. _____

Solutions on page 170

Carrie Fisher

Find 7 five-letter words:

1. _____
2. _____
3. _____
4. _____
5. _____
6. _____
7. _____

Golda Meir

Find 7 five-letter words:

1. _____
2. _____
3. _____
4. _____
5. _____
6. _____
7. _____

Liam Neeson

Find 7 five-letter words:

1. _____
2. _____
3. _____
4. _____
5. _____
6. _____
7. _____

Dean Martin

Find 7 five-letter words:

1. _____
2. _____
3. _____
4. _____
5. _____
6. _____
7. _____

Solutions on pages 171–172

Frankie Valli

Find 7 five-letter words:

1. _____
2. _____
3. _____
4. _____
5. _____
6. _____
7. _____

Kurt Cobain

Find 7 five-letter words:

1. _____
2. _____
3. _____
4. _____
5. _____
6. _____
7. _____

Petula Clark

Find 7 five-letter words:

1. _____
2. _____
3. _____
4. _____
5. _____
6. _____
7. _____

Stephen King

Find 7 five-letter words:

1. _____
2. _____
3. _____
4. _____
5. _____
6. _____
7. _____

Solutions on pages 172–173

Pablo Picasso

Find 7 five-letter words:

1. _____
2. _____
3. _____
4. _____
5. _____
6. _____
7. _____

Solutions on page 173

Word Ladders

Link these word pairs together with a ladder of words. Each step in the ladder must be a real word and must differ from the previous word by only one letter. For example, CAT can be linked to DOG with these steps: CAT, COT, DOT, DOG. There are many possible solutions for these puzzles, but try to use only the given number of steps.

BOY to MAN

B   O   Y

___   ___   ___

___   ___   ___

M   A   N

AIR to ART

A   I   R

___   ___   ___

___   ___   ___

A   R   T

CAR to TOY

C   A   R

___   ___   ___

___   ___   ___

___   ___   ___

T   O   Y

PIG to HAM

P   I   G

___   ___   ___

___   ___   ___

___   ___   ___

H   A   M

LOG to OAR

L   O   G

___   ___   ___

___   ___   ___

___   ___   ___

O   A   R

BEE to WAX

B   E   E

___   ___   ___

___   ___   ___

___   ___   ___

W   A   X

Solutions on pages 173–174

FOX to DEN

F O X

___ ___ ___

___ ___ ___

___ ___ ___

D E N

EAT to ATE

E A T

___ ___ ___

___ ___ ___

___ ___ ___

A T E

DOC to FLU

D O C

___ ___ ___

___ ___ ___

___ ___ ___

F L U

EGG TO HEN

E G G

___ ___ ___

___ ___ ___

___ ___ ___

___ ___ ___

___ ___ ___

___ ___ ___

H E N

TIME to BELL

T I M E

___ ___ ___ ___

B E L L

SING to TONE

S I N G

___ ___ ___ ___

___ ___ ___ ___

T O N E

Solutions on page 174

COAT to SHOE

C   O   A   T

___ ___ ___ ___

___ ___ ___ ___

___ ___ ___ ___

S   H   O   E

SEND to HOME

S   E   N   D

___ ___ ___ ___

___ ___ ___ ___

___ ___ ___ ___

H   O   M   E

POND to LAKE

P   O   N   D

___ ___ ___ ___

___ ___ ___ ___

L   A   K   E

PLAY to GROW

P   L   A   Y

___ ___ ___ ___

___ ___ ___ ___

___ ___ ___ ___

G   R   O   W

BOOK to FILM

B   O   O   K

___ ___ ___ ___

___ ___ ___ ___

___ ___ ___ ___

F   I   L   M

ZERO to FREE

Z   E   R   O

___ ___ ___ ___

___ ___ ___ ___

___ ___ ___ ___

___ ___ ___ ___

___ ___ ___ ___

F   R   E   E

Solutions on page 175

TOWN to CITY

T O W N
___ ___ ___ ___
___ ___ ___ ___
___ ___ ___ ___
___ ___ ___ ___
C I T Y

KISS to TELL

K I S S
___ ___ ___ ___
___ ___ ___ ___
___ ___ ___ ___
___ ___ ___ ___
T E L L

SIREN to FADES

S I R E N
___ ___ ___ ___ ___
___ ___ ___ ___ ___
F A D E S

PAPER to GAMES

P A P E R
___ ___ ___ ___ ___
___ ___ ___ ___ ___
G A M E S

MOUSE to WORST

M O U S E
___ ___ ___ ___ ___
___ ___ ___ ___ ___
W O R S T

CLUMP to TRASH

C L U M P
___ ___ ___ ___ ___
___ ___ ___ ___ ___
___ ___ ___ ___ ___
T R A S H

Solutions on pages 175–176

START to PHONE

```
S   T   A   R   T
__  __  __  __  __
__  __  __  __  __
__  __  __  __  __
P   H   O   N   E
```

WATER to PALES

```
W   A   T   E   R
__  __  __  __  __
__  __  __  __  __
P   A   L   E   S
```

OUTER to BAKED

```
O   U   T   E   R
__  __  __  __  __
__  __  __  __  __
__  __  __  __  __
B   A   K   E   D
```

TIGER to MATED

```
T   I   G   E   R
__  __  __  __  __
__  __  __  __  __
__  __  __  __  __
M   A   T   E   D
```

Solutions on page 176

Answers

Chapter 2: **Crossword Puzzles**

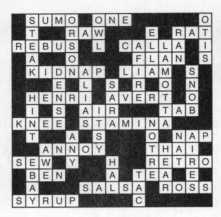

Crossword Puzzle 1

Crossword Puzzle 2

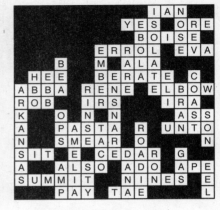

Crossword Puzzle 3

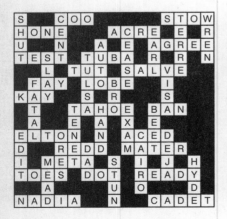

Crossword Puzzle 4

Crossword Puzzle 5

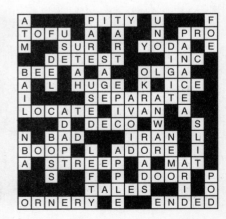

Crossword Puzzle 6

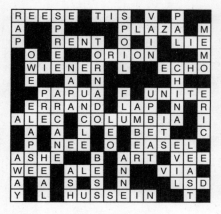

Crossword Puzzle 7

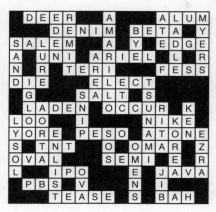

Crossword Puzzle 8

Crossword Puzzle 9

Crossword Puzzle 10

Crossword Puzzle 11

Crossword Puzzle 12

ANSWERS • 143

Crossword Puzzle 13

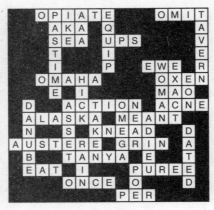

Crossword Puzzle 14

Crossword Puzzle 15

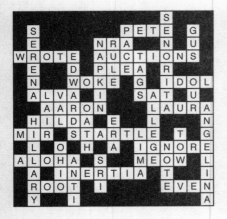

Crossword Puzzle 16

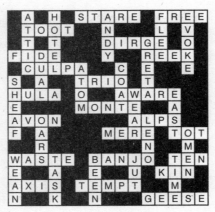

Crossword Puzzle 17

Chapter 3: **Sudoku Puzzles**

Sudoku Puzzle 1

8	9	2	7	1	5	6	3	4
4	1	5	3	9	6	7	2	8
3	7	6	4	2	8	9	5	1
7	6	8	2	5	9	1	4	3
9	4	1	8	3	7	2	6	5
2	5	3	6	4	1	8	9	7
6	8	9	5	7	3	4	1	2
1	3	4	9	8	2	5	7	6
5	2	7	1	6	4	3	8	9

Sudoku Puzzle 2

3	4	9	8	2	6	5	7	1
1	5	8	4	7	3	9	2	6
7	6	2	5	9	1	8	4	3
9	8	4	1	5	2	6	3	7
2	3	1	7	6	8	4	9	5
5	7	6	9	3	4	2	1	8
8	2	3	6	4	7	1	5	9
6	9	7	2	1	5	3	8	4
4	1	5	3	8	9	7	6	2

Sudoku Puzzle 3

9	2	3	4	5	6	8	7	1
8	5	1	9	3	7	4	6	2
7	6	4	2	1	8	9	3	5
1	7	2	8	9	5	3	4	6
6	3	8	1	4	2	7	5	9
4	9	5	7	6	3	1	2	8
5	8	9	3	2	4	6	1	7
2	4	7	6	8	1	5	9	3
3	1	6	5	7	9	2	8	4

Sudoku Puzzle 4

5	1	6	3	2	8	4	9	7
7	3	9	1	6	4	2	8	5
8	4	2	7	9	5	1	6	3
3	6	4	8	7	1	5	2	9
9	5	8	2	4	6	3	7	1
2	7	1	9	5	3	8	4	6
4	8	7	5	3	9	6	1	2
6	9	3	4	1	2	7	5	8
1	2	5	6	8	7	9	3	4

Sudoku Puzzle 5

6	1	9	8	7	5	2	4	3
2	7	4	6	3	9	5	8	1
3	8	5	4	2	1	9	6	7
1	5	3	9	4	2	6	7	8
8	2	6	7	1	3	4	5	9
4	9	7	5	8	6	3	1	2
5	3	2	1	6	7	8	9	4
7	6	8	2	9	4	1	3	5
9	4	1	3	5	8	7	2	6

Sudoku Puzzle 6

8	3	7	9	6	2	4	1	5
9	5	6	7	1	4	8	3	2
2	1	4	8	5	3	7	6	9
5	8	3	4	7	9	6	2	1
1	7	2	5	8	6	9	4	3
4	6	9	3	2	1	5	8	7
7	9	1	2	4	8	3	5	6
6	4	5	1	3	7	2	9	8
3	2	8	6	9	5	1	7	4

Sudoku Puzzle 7

1	5	9	3	7	6	2	8	4
7	3	4	8	9	2	6	1	5
6	2	8	4	5	1	3	7	9
8	1	5	7	6	9	4	2	3
9	7	3	5	2	4	8	6	1
2	4	6	1	3	8	9	5	7
4	9	1	6	8	7	5	3	2
3	8	7	2	4	5	1	9	6
5	6	2	9	1	3	7	4	8

Sudoku Puzzle 8

4	9	1	2	3	7	6	5	8
5	6	2	4	9	8	3	1	7
3	7	8	6	1	5	4	9	2
9	4	3	7	8	1	2	6	5
8	2	6	5	4	3	9	7	1
7	1	5	9	2	6	8	3	4
1	8	7	3	6	2	5	4	9
2	3	9	1	5	4	7	8	6
6	5	4	8	7	9	1	2	3

Sudoku Puzzle 9

1	5	8	4	6	3	7	2	9
3	4	7	9	2	5	8	1	6
2	9	6	1	7	8	4	5	3
5	6	2	7	9	4	1	3	8
4	8	3	5	1	6	9	7	2
7	1	9	3	8	2	5	6	4
6	7	1	8	3	9	2	4	5
9	2	4	6	5	1	3	8	7
8	3	5	2	4	7	6	9	1

Sudoku Puzzle 10

6	3	5	9	2	4	1	7	8
8	7	4	6	1	5	3	2	9
1	9	2	3	8	7	6	5	4
5	4	1	8	6	3	2	9	7
9	2	7	5	4	1	8	6	3
3	8	6	7	9	2	5	4	1
7	1	3	4	5	6	9	8	2
4	6	9	2	3	8	7	1	5
2	5	8	1	7	9	4	3	6

Sudoku Puzzle 11

6	7	9	5	4	1	8	2	3
1	5	2	8	3	9	6	7	4
4	8	3	2	6	7	9	5	1
5	3	4	1	9	2	7	8	6
9	1	8	6	7	3	5	4	2
7	2	6	4	5	8	1	3	9
3	6	7	9	8	4	2	1	5
2	4	5	7	1	6	3	9	8
8	9	1	3	2	5	4	6	7

Sudoku Puzzle 12

1	6	3	2	4	5	9	7	8
9	4	8	6	7	3	1	2	5
7	5	2	8	9	1	4	3	6
3	7	5	4	1	6	2	8	9
4	8	6	9	2	7	3	5	1
2	1	9	5	3	8	6	4	7
5	3	7	1	6	4	8	9	2
8	2	1	3	5	9	7	6	4
6	9	4	7	8	2	5	1	3

Sudoku Puzzle 13

6	5	4	9	1	7	8	3	2
1	3	2	8	6	4	5	9	7
7	8	9	2	3	5	1	4	6
9	2	7	3	5	1	4	6	8
5	4	1	6	9	8	7	2	3
8	6	3	4	7	2	9	1	5
2	7	5	1	4	6	3	8	9
3	1	8	5	2	9	6	7	4
4	9	6	7	8	3	2	5	1

Sudoku Puzzle 14

5	3	1	2	9	6	4	8	7
9	2	4	3	8	7	6	5	1
7	8	6	4	1	5	3	9	2
4	7	5	9	3	1	8	2	6
3	9	2	7	6	8	5	1	4
6	1	8	5	2	4	7	3	9
2	5	9	6	4	3	1	7	8
8	6	7	1	5	2	9	4	3
1	4	3	8	7	9	2	6	5

Sudoku Puzzle 15

1	9	4	7	8	5	2	6	3
3	8	7	4	2	6	5	9	1
6	2	5	9	1	3	4	7	8
8	3	6	1	5	4	7	2	9
9	4	1	2	6	7	8	3	5
5	7	2	8	3	9	1	4	6
2	6	3	5	7	1	9	8	4
4	1	8	3	9	2	6	5	7
7	5	9	6	4	8	3	1	2

Sudoku Puzzle 16

5	8	7	2	4	1	3	9	6
2	6	4	5	3	9	1	7	8
3	1	9	6	8	7	2	5	4
9	5	6	8	2	4	7	1	3
4	2	1	7	9	3	8	6	5
7	3	8	1	5	6	4	2	9
8	7	3	9	6	2	5	4	1
6	4	2	3	1	5	9	8	7
1	9	5	4	7	8	6	3	2

Sudoku Puzzle 17

4	1	2	6	8	5	3	7	9
6	3	7	9	4	1	2	8	5
9	8	5	7	2	3	4	6	1
8	2	9	4	1	7	5	3	6
7	6	4	3	5	2	1	9	8
3	5	1	8	6	9	7	2	4
5	9	6	2	7	4	8	1	3
1	7	8	5	3	6	9	4	2
2	4	3	1	9	8	6	5	7

Sudoku Puzzle 18

7	1	3	9	5	4	6	8	2
6	8	4	2	1	7	5	9	3
9	5	2	8	6	3	1	7	4
3	9	1	5	4	8	2	6	7
8	4	7	6	2	1	3	5	9
2	6	5	3	7	9	4	1	8
5	2	9	7	3	6	8	4	1
1	7	6	4	8	2	9	3	5
4	3	8	1	9	5	7	2	6

Sudoku Puzzle 19

1	8	4	9	5	2	6	3	7
5	7	3	1	6	4	8	9	2
6	2	9	8	3	7	5	1	4
2	4	8	7	1	5	3	6	9
3	6	5	4	8	9	2	7	1
7	9	1	3	2	6	4	5	8
8	5	2	6	7	1	9	4	3
9	3	7	5	4	8	1	2	6
4	1	6	2	9	3	7	8	5

Sudoku Puzzle 20

9	4	7	3	2	6	8	1	5
6	3	1	7	5	8	4	2	9
2	8	5	4	1	9	3	6	7
5	6	8	2	7	3	9	4	1
1	9	3	8	6	4	5	7	2
7	2	4	1	9	5	6	8	3
3	1	9	6	4	2	7	5	8
4	5	2	9	8	7	1	3	6
8	7	6	5	3	1	2	9	4

Sudoku Puzzle 21

5	7	3	9	1	2	8	6	4
2	4	1	8	6	7	9	5	3
6	9	8	4	5	3	7	2	1
7	5	6	1	8	4	3	9	2
4	3	9	2	7	5	6	1	8
1	8	2	3	9	6	5	4	7
8	2	5	6	3	1	4	7	9
9	1	7	5	4	8	2	3	6
3	6	4	7	2	9	1	8	5

Sudoku Puzzle 22

1	8	9	5	3	2	7	4	6
4	7	5	9	6	8	2	3	1
2	3	6	4	1	7	9	5	8
6	5	2	1	8	9	4	7	3
8	4	1	3	7	5	6	9	2
3	9	7	6	2	4	8	1	5
9	6	4	2	5	3	1	8	7
7	1	3	8	4	6	5	2	9
5	2	8	7	9	1	3	6	4

Sudoku Puzzle 23

2	6	7	5	8	1	4	9	3
1	3	8	9	6	4	7	5	2
9	4	5	7	3	2	1	6	8
4	5	3	6	7	9	2	8	1
6	7	2	1	4	8	5	3	9
8	9	1	3	2	5	6	4	7
7	1	4	8	9	6	3	2	5
5	2	9	4	1	3	8	7	6
3	8	6	2	5	7	9	1	4

Sudoku Puzzle 24

7	1	2	3	9	5	4	6	8
3	6	9	8	2	4	5	1	7
8	4	5	7	1	6	2	3	9
1	7	6	9	4	2	8	5	3
4	5	3	6	8	1	7	9	2
9	2	8	5	3	7	6	4	1
5	3	1	4	7	8	9	2	6
2	8	4	1	6	9	3	7	5
6	9	7	2	5	3	1	8	4

Sudoku Puzzle 25

6	5	9	4	2	1	8	7	3
4	7	2	3	6	8	5	9	1
1	3	8	9	7	5	6	2	4
2	1	3	5	9	7	4	6	8
9	8	6	2	3	4	1	5	7
7	4	5	8	1	6	9	3	2
8	9	7	1	5	2	3	4	6
5	2	4	6	8	3	7	1	9
3	6	1	7	4	9	2	8	5

Sudoku Puzzle 26

3	6	8	7	1	5	9	2	4
9	5	1	2	6	4	7	8	3
7	2	4	3	8	9	1	6	5
2	7	6	5	4	1	3	9	8
8	4	9	6	3	7	5	1	2
1	3	5	9	2	8	4	7	6
5	8	3	1	9	2	6	4	7
6	1	2	4	7	3	8	5	9
4	9	7	8	5	6	2	3	1

Sudoku Puzzle 27

1	2	8	7	4	9	3	5	6
7	4	6	5	3	2	8	1	9
5	3	9	6	1	8	4	7	2
9	1	3	4	7	6	2	8	5
6	5	2	8	9	1	7	3	4
8	7	4	3	2	5	6	9	1
2	8	7	9	5	4	1	6	3
3	9	1	2	6	7	5	4	8
4	6	5	1	8	3	9	2	7

Sudoku Puzzle 28

7	1	6	3	4	2	5	9	8
8	5	3	1	9	7	4	2	6
9	4	2	5	8	6	1	7	3
1	3	7	9	6	8	2	5	4
5	2	4	7	3	1	6	8	9
6	8	9	2	5	4	7	3	1
4	7	5	8	1	3	9	6	2
2	6	8	4	7	9	3	1	5
3	9	1	6	2	5	8	4	7

Sudoku Puzzle 29

7	4	5	8	3	1	6	9	2
1	6	3	4	2	9	7	5	8
2	9	8	5	7	6	1	3	4
8	3	7	2	6	5	9	4	1
4	1	6	7	9	3	8	2	5
5	2	9	1	8	4	3	7	6
3	5	2	9	1	8	4	6	7
6	7	1	3	4	2	5	8	9
9	8	4	6	5	7	2	1	3

Sudoku Puzzle 30

2	8	3	4	1	7	9	5	6
1	6	5	3	9	8	4	7	2
4	7	9	5	6	2	8	1	3
5	2	7	9	8	4	6	3	1
6	1	4	7	3	5	2	9	8
9	3	8	6	2	1	7	4	5
8	5	2	1	4	9	3	6	7
7	4	6	2	5	3	1	8	9
3	9	1	8	7	6	5	2	4

Sudoku Puzzle 31

7	1	2	9	3	4	8	5	6
5	8	6	1	7	2	9	4	3
9	4	3	6	5	8	2	7	1
1	6	5	2	8	9	4	3	7
3	9	7	4	1	5	6	2	8
4	2	8	3	6	7	5	1	9
6	5	1	8	4	3	7	9	2
8	7	9	5	2	1	3	6	4
2	3	4	7	9	6	1	8	5

Sudoku Puzzle 32

2	4	5	6	9	3	7	8	1
6	3	1	7	8	5	2	4	9
9	8	7	4	1	2	5	6	3
7	2	6	5	4	9	3	1	8
4	1	3	8	2	7	6	9	5
5	9	8	3	6	1	4	2	7
3	6	9	1	7	4	8	5	2
1	5	4	2	3	8	9	7	6
8	7	2	9	5	6	1	3	4

Sudoku Puzzle 33

5	9	6	2	1	7	3	8	4
2	3	8	4	6	9	5	7	1
1	7	4	8	5	3	2	9	6
4	6	7	5	3	1	9	2	8
3	5	2	9	8	6	1	4	7
8	1	9	7	2	4	6	5	3
6	8	5	3	7	2	4	1	9
9	2	1	6	4	8	7	3	5
7	4	3	1	9	5	8	6	2

Chapter 4: **Word Search Puzzles**

Countries

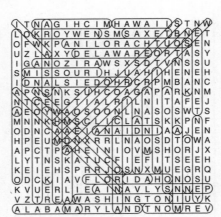

United States

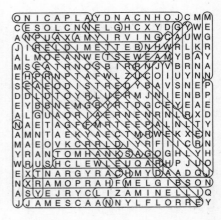

At the Movies

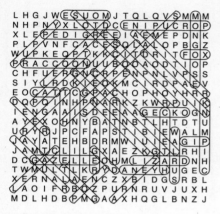

Land Creatures

Water Creatures

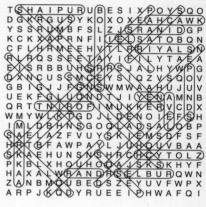

Money

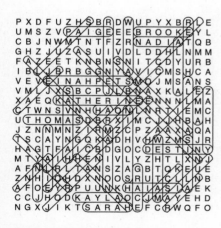

Naming Names

U.S. Presidents

The Periodic Table

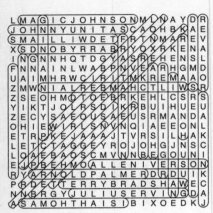

Athletes

How's the Weather

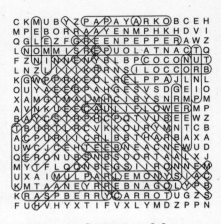

Fruits and Vegetables

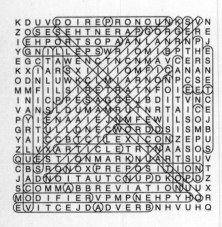

Grammatical

U.S. National Parks

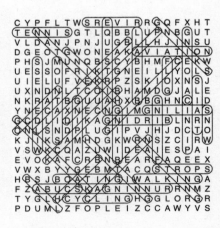

Outdoor Fun

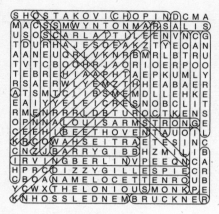

Musical People

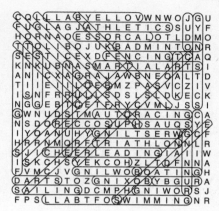

Sports

Chapter 5: **Mazes**

Rectangle 1

Rectangle 2

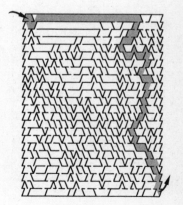

Rectangle 3

Concentric 1

Concentric 2

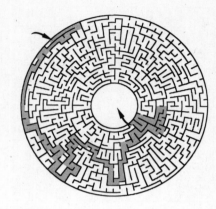

Concentric 3

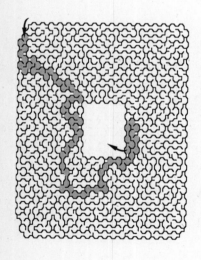

Break In

Break Out

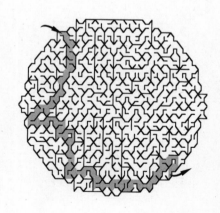

Circle

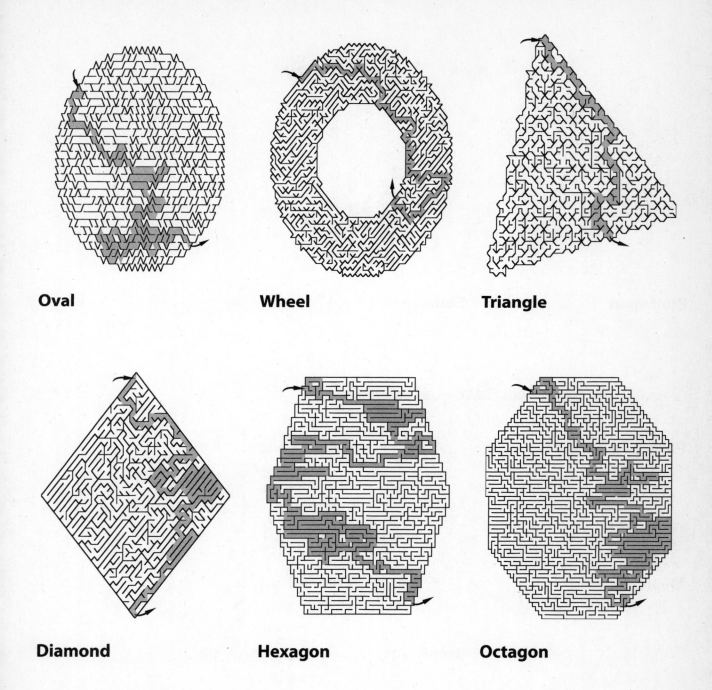

Oval

Wheel

Triangle

Diamond

Hexagon

Octagon

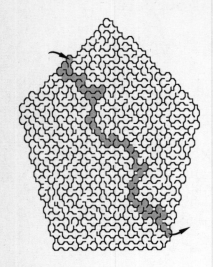

Pentagon

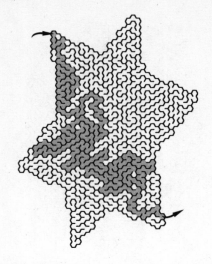

Star

Chapter 6: **Scrambled Categories**

Parts of a Book

1. SPINE
2. PAGES
3. COVER
4. JACKET
5. BINDING

Musical

1. TRUMPET
2. GUITAR
3. PIANO
4. DRUM
5. VIOLIN

Bake a Cake

1. FLOUR
2. SUGAR
3. EGGS
4. BUTTER
5. MILK

Colorful

1. PURPLE
2. YELLOW
3. GREEN
4. ORANGE
5. BROWN

Things in the Kitchen

1. SPATULA
2. KNIFE
3. OVEN
4. BLENDER
5. REFRIGERATOR

Things in the Workshop

1. SCREWDRIVER
2. HAMMER
3. WRENCH
4. DRILL
5. PLIERS

What Does Your Garden Grow?

1. CORN
2. SQUASH
3. TOMATOES
4. CARROTS
5. WATERMELON

On the Water

1. CANOE
2. KAYAK
3. SAILBOAT
4. MOTORBOAT
5. RAFT

The Shirt on Your Back

1. BUTTON
2. COLLAR
3. SLEEVE
4. POCKET
5. FABRIC

Auto Parts

1. TIRES
2. ENGINE
3. BRAKES
4. MUFFLER
5. WINDSHIELD

Legal Words

1. JUDGE
2. ATTORNEY
3. WITNESS
4. JURY
5. COURT

Electronic

1. RADIO
2. TELEVISION
3. COMPUTER
4. MICROWAVE
5. STEREO

Sports

1. BASKETBALL
2. BASEBALL
3. FOOTBALL
4. HOCKEY
5. SOCCER

Out of This World

1. PLUTO
2. JUPITER
3. VENUS
4. SATURN
5. MERCURY

Halloween Costumes

1. WITCH
2. GHOST
3. PRINCESS
4. MONSTER
5. PIRATE

Drive Through

1. STREET
2. AVENUE
3. DRIVE
4. HIGHWAY
5. PARKWAY

Make Haste

1. QUICK
2. SPEEDY
3. PROMPT
4. RAPID
5. SWIFT

Drawing Tools

1. PAINTBRUSH
2. MARKER
3. PENCIL
4. CRAYON
5. CHALK

Things in the Bathroom

1. TOILET
2. BATHTUB
3. SINK
4. MIRROR
5. SHOWER

Literary Genres

1. MYSTERY
2. ROMANCE
3. POETRY
4. NOVELS
5. CLASSICS

Star Sign

1. CAPRICORN
2. SCORPIO
3. AQUARIUS
4. SAGITTARIUS
5. TAURUS

Family Life

1. GRANDMA
2. AUNT
3. COUSIN
4. UNCLE
5. BROTHER

Tree Parts

1. TRUNK
2. LEAVES
3. ROOTS
4. BRANCHES
5. BARK

Water

1. RESERVOIR
2. POND
3. RIVER
4. STREAM
5. CREEK

Computer System

1. MEMORY
2. MONITOR
3. PRINTER
4. KEYBOARD
5. MOUSE

Land Features

1. MOUNTAIN
2. VALLEY
3. CANYON
4. VOLCANO
5. PLATEAU

Wedding

1. BRIDE
2. GROOM
3. HONEYMOON
4. MARRIAGE
5. ENGAGEMENT

Parts of a Bicycle

1. HANDLEBAR
2. CHAIN
3. PEDALS
4. BRAKES
5. SADDLE

Cheese Please

1. CHEDDAR
2. GOUDA
3. SWISS
4. AMERICAN
5. MOZZARELLA

Home Sweet Home

1. ABODE
2. RESIDENCE
3. APARTMENT
4. DWELLING
5. CONDOMINIUM

Bakery Treats

1. CROISSANT
2. BREAD
3. DOUGHNUT
4. MUFFIN
5. SCONE

Chessmen

1. PAWN
2. ROOK
3. KNIGHT
4. BISHOP
5. QUEEN

Card Games

1. POKER
2. BRIDGE
3. RUMMY
4. SOLITAIRE
5. BLACKJACK

Chapter 7: *Triplet Puzzles*

Triplet 1

BRUSH: toothbrush, brush up, paintbrush

Triplet 2

CUP: buttercup, cupcake, suction cup

Triplet 3

PAPER: paper clip, paperback, newspaper

Triplet 4

HEART: heartache, artichoke heart, heartworm

Triplet 5

WILL: goodwill, willpower, living will

Triplet 6

BELLY: belly dance, belly button, pork belly

Triplet 7

WOOD: driftwood, woodchuck, redwood

Triplet 8

SHORT: shortcake, shortstop, shortwave

Triplet 9

NOTE: notebook, keynote, noteworthy

Triplet 10

LIGHT: light bulb, flashlight, moonlight

Triplet 11

SHOW: showdown, game show, showcase

Triplet 12

STOP: pit stop, stopgap, stopwatch

Triplet 13

OUT: blackout, outcast, breakout

Triplet 14

PEN: fountain pen, pen pal, bullpen

Triplet 15

CELL: stem cell, cell phone, cancer cell

Triplet 16

BREAD: white bread, breadwinner, breadstick

Triplet 17

TIME: bedtime, Christmastime, timekeeper

Triplet 18

HAND: backhand, firsthand, handheld

Triplet 19

BELL: bell-bottom, bluebell, dumbbell

Triplet 20

CHAIR: easy chair, chairman, highchair

Triplet 21

WHEEL: wheelchair, big wheel, cartwheel

Triplet 22

FOUR: fourscore, four-wheeler, four-eyes

Triplet 23

FLOOR: dance floor, floor plan, ground floor

Triplet 24

BALL: basketball, ballpoint, cornball

Triplet 25

UP: blowup, uproar, cleanup

Triplet 26

CHECK: checkbook, paycheck, checkmate

Triplet 27

BOARD: blackboard, boardroom, surfboard

Triplet 28

WASH: brainwash, washcloth, whitewash

Triplet 29

MOUTH: badmouth, mouthwash, loudmouth

Triplet 30

HONEY: honeymoon, honeydew, honeybee

Triplet 31

TAIL: coattail, tailgate, cottontail

Triplet 32

BREAK: breakneck, spring break, heartbreak

Triplet 33

DROP: raindrop, dropkick, gumdrop

Triplet 34

EYE: bull's-eye, eyewitness, eyeball

Triplet 35

TOOTH: toothpaste, sweet tooth, toothpick

Triplet 36

DOG: hotdog, dogwood, bulldog

Triplet 37

FIRE: ceasefire, firecracker, wildfire

Triplet 38

COFFEE: coffee bean, coffee table, coffee break

Triplet 39

LAND: landmark, landlocked, Iceland

Triplet 40

POLE: pole vault, fishing pole, north pole

Triplet 41

SHIP: flagship, shipshape, spaceship

Triplet 42

POWER: power trip, horsepower, power grid

Triplet 43

FREE: freeloader, carefree, freehand

Triplet 44

HOLD: stranglehold, holdup, household

Triplet 45

BODY: bodyguard, busybody, somebody

Triplet 46

WORK: homework, workbench, patchwork

Triplet 47

POINT: needlepoint, viewpoint, pinpoint

Triplet 48

CARD: flashcard, cardboard, postcard

Triplet 49

FRY: stir-fry, small fry, French fry

Triplet 50

HOUR: happy hour, hourglass, rush hour

Triplet 51

LITTLE: little dipper, chicken little, little league

Triplet 52

STREAM: bloodstream, mainstream, streamline

Triplet 53

COLD: common cold, cold cuts, cold shoulder

Triplet 54

RING: brass ring, ringworm, wedding ring

Triplet 55

PLATE: boilerplate, plate glass, paper plate

Triplet 56

LINE: linebacker, clothesline, borderline

Triplet 57

BASE: base station, home base, database

Triplet 58

PAGE: home page, page-turner, pageboy

Triplet 59

BACK: background, backpack, horseback

Triplet 60

STEP: stepladder, footstep, stepmother

Triplet 61

BOX: box office, soapbox, mailbox

Triplet 62

ZONE: combat zone, end zone, comfort zone

Triplet 63

PLAY: playground, playmate, wordplay

Triplet 64

PACK: six-pack, backpack, pack rat

Triplet 65

MAIL: mailbox, junk mail, blackmail

Triplet 66

BOOK: bookmarker, bookkeeper, yearbook

Triplet 67

STAR: starfish, superstar, stardust

Triplet 68

LETTER: scarlet letter, letterhead, love letter

Triplet 69

STOCK: laughingstock, Woodstock, stockbroker

Triplet 70

HOME: homecoming, motor home, homemaker

Triplet 71

ROOM: bathroom, roommate, classroom

Triplet 72

DUST: dust cover, sawdust, dust storm

Triplet 73

LIFE: lifesaver, wildlife, lifestyle

Triplet 74

CRY: cry wolf, battle cry, crybaby

Triplet 75

DOWN: countdown, meltdown, downstairs

Triplet 76

FLASH: flashbulb, newsflash, flashback

Triplet 77

PHOTO: photocopy, photo finish, photojournalism

Triplet 78

WATER: watermelon, dishwater, waterproof

Triplet 79

DUCK: lame duck, duck soup, sitting duck

Triplet 80

GIRL: flower girl, girl scout, girl Friday

Triplet 81

SHOP: shoplifter, barbershop, window-shop

Triplet 82

PARK: parallel park, parkway, trailer park

Triplet 83

END: end table, end zone, bitter end

Chapter 8: *What's in a Name?*

Chris Evert

cees, cere, cete, chis, chit, cire, cist, cite, cris, eche, errs, erst, etch, eths, etic, ever, eves, heir, here, hers, hest, hets, hies, hire, hist, hits, hive, ices, ichs, ires, itch, recs, rees, reis, resh, rest, rete, rets, revs, rice, rich, rise, rite, rive, sect, seer, sere, shiv, shri, sice, sire, site, sith, stir, tees, thee, thir, this, tics, tier, ties, tire, tree, veer, vees, vert, vest, vets, vice, vier, vies, vise

Jacques Cousteau

aces, acta, acts, ajee, aqua, asea, ates, auto, caca, casa, case, cast, cate, cats, ceca, cees, cess, cete, coat, coca, coss, cost, cote, cots, cues, cuss, cute, cuts, ease, east, eats, ecus, eses, etas, jato, jees, jess, jest, jete, jets, joes, joss, jota, jots, just, jute, juts, oast, oats, ocas, oses, ossa, oust, outs, qats, sacs, sate, scat, scot, scut, seas, seat, secs, sect, sees, seta, sets, soja, sots, sous, stoa, sues, suet, suqs, tace, taco, taos, tass, taus, teas, tees, toea, toes, toss, uses, utas

Fred MacMurray

aced, acme, acre, aery, afar, area, army, arum, aura, cade, cafe, came, card, care, carr, cram, crud, cued, curd, cure, curf, curr, cyma, cyme, dace, dame, dare, deaf, dear, defy, demy, derm, dram, dray, drum, duce, duma, dura, dure, durr, dyer, ecru, emyd, eyra, face, fade, fame, fard, fare, farm, fear, feud, frae, fray, fume, fumy, fury, fyce, maar, mace, made, mama, marc, mare, maud, maya, mead, mura, mure, murr, race, racy, rare, raya, read, ream, rear, rude, rued, ruer, urea, yard, yare, yaud, year, yuca

Richard Gere

aced, ache, acid, acre, aged, agee, ager, aide, arch, arid, cade, cadi, cage, caid, card, care, carr, cede, cedi, cere, chad, char, chia, chid, cire, crag, dace, dare, dear, deer, dere, dice, dire, drag, dree, dreg, each, eche, edge, egad, eger, eide, gadi, gaed, gear, geed, ghee, gied, gird, grad, gree, grid, hade, haed, hair, hard, hare, head, hear, heed, heir, herd, here, hide, hied, hire, iced, idea, ired, race, rage, ragi, raid, rare, read, rear, rede, reed, rhea, rice, rich, ride

Ginger Rogers

eger, eggs, egis, egos, engs, eons, ergo, ergs, erne, erns, eros, errs, gees, gene, gens, gien, gies, gigs, gins, girn, giro, goer, goes, gone, gong, gore, gree, grig, grin, grog, inro, ions, ires, iron, noes, nogg, nogs, noir, nori, nose, ogee, ogre, ones, ores, rees, regs, rein, reis, rigs, ring, rins, rise, roes, rose, seen, seer, sego, sene, sere, sign, sine, sing, sire, snog, sone, song, sore, sori, sorn

J. Edgar Hoover

aero, aged, agee, ager, ajee, arvo, aver, dago, dare, dear, deer, dere, deva, doer, doge, dojo, door, dore, dorr, dove, drag, dree, dreg, eave, edge, egad, eger, ergo, ever, gaed, gave, gear, geed, ghee, goad, goer, good, gore, grad, gree, hade, hadj, haed, hard, hare, have, head, hear, heed, herd, here, hero, hoar, hoed, hoer, hood, hora, hove, jade, jeed, jeer, odea, odor, ogee, ogre, ohed, orad, ordo, orra, over, rage, rare, rave, read, rear, rede, redo, reed, rhea, road, roar, rode, rood, rove, veer, vera

Cat Stevens

aces, acne, acts, anes, ante, ants, ates, aves, cane, cans, cant, case, cast, cate, cats, cave, cees, cent, cess, cete, ease, east, eats, eave, eses, etas, etna, even, eves, nave, neat, ness, nest, nets, nett, neve, sacs, sane, sans, sate, save, scan, scat, seas, seat, secs, sect, seen, sees, sene, sent, seta, sets, sett, stat, stet, tace, tact, tans, tass, tate, tats, tavs, teas, teat, teen, tees, tens, tent, test, tets, vacs, vane, vans, vase, vast, vats, vees, vena, vent, vest, vets

Sam Donaldson

aals, adds, ados, alan, alas, alma, alms, also, amas, anal, anas, ands, anna, anoa, anon, ansa, dada, dado, dads, dals, damn, dams, dodo, dols, doms, dona, dons, doom, doss, lads, lama, lams, land, lass, load, loam, loan, loom, loon, loos, loss, mads, mana, mano, mans, mass, moan, moas, mods, mola, mold, mols, mono, mons, mood, mool, moon, moos, moss, naan, nada, nana, nans, naos, nods, nolo, noma, noms, nona, noon, odds, olds, ossa, sals, sand, sans, slam, soda, sods, sola, sold, solo, sols, soma, sons, soon

Jason Robards

abas, abos, ados, ajar, anas, ands, anoa, ansa, arbs, baas, bads, band, bans, bard, barn, bars, bass, boar, boas, bods, bond, boon, boor, boos, bora, born, boss, brad, bran, bras, broo, bros, dabs, darb, darn, dojo, dona, dons, door, dorr, dors, doss, drab, jabs, jars, jobs, joss, nabs, nada, naos, nard, nobs, nods, oars, odor, orad, orbs, ordo, orra, osar, ossa, rads, raja, rand, road, roan, roar, robs, rods, rood, sabs, sand, sans, sard, snob, soar, sobs, soda, sods, soja, sons, soon, sora, sorb, sord, sorn

Farrah Fawcett

ache, acre, acta, afar, arch, area, cafe, caff, care, carr, cart, cate, char, chat, chaw, chef, chew, craw, crew, each, eath, etch, face, fact, fare, fart, fate, fear, feat, feta, frae, frat, fret, haaf, haar, haet, haft, hare, hart, hate, hear, heat, heft, race, raff, raft, rare, rate, rath, rear, reft, rhea, tace, tach, tact, tahr, tare, tart, tate, tear, teat, teff, teth, thae, that, thaw, thew, tref, tret, twae, twat, waff, waft, ware, wart, watt, wear, weft, wert, what, whet

Keanu Reeves

akee, anes, anus, ares, arks, arse, auks, aver, aves, earn, ears, ease, eave, ekes, eras, erne, erns, even, ever, eves, kaes, kane, karn, keas, keen, kens, kern, knar, knee, knur, kues, kvas, nark, nave, near, neuk, neve, nuke, rake, rank, rase, rave, reek, rees, revs, rues, rune, runs, ruse, rusk, sake, sane, sank, sark, save, sear, seek, seen, seer, sene, sera, sere, skee, skua, suer, sunk, sura, sure, ukes, urea, urns, ursa, user, uvea, vane, vans, vars, vase, vaus, veer, vees, vena, vera

Conan O'Brien

abri, acne, acre, aeon, aero, airn, anon, arco, bane, bani, bare, barn, bean, bear, bice, bier, bine, boar, bone, boon, boor, bora, bore, born, brae, bran, bren, brie, brin, brio, broo, cain, cane, carb, care, carn, cero, ciao, cine, cion, cire, coin, coir, cone, coni, conn, coon, core, corn, crab, crib, earn, ebon, icon, inro, iron, nabe, naoi, narc, near, neon, nice, nine, noir, nona, none, noon, nori, obia, oboe, once, orca, race, rain, rani, rein, rice, roan, robe

James Baker

abas, ajar, ajee, akee, amas, arak, arbs, area, ares, arks, arms, arse, asea, baas, bake, bams, bare, bark, barm, bars, base, bask, beak, beam, bear, beer, bees, bema, berm, brae, bras, bree, ears, ease, ekes, emes, eras, jabs, jake, jamb, jams, jars, jeer, jees, jerk, kaas, kabs, kaes, kame, kbar, keas, kerb, maar, mabe, maes, make, mare, mark, mars, mask, meek, mere, merk, mesa, raja, rake, rams, rase, ream, rebs, reek, rees, rems, sabe, sake, same, sark, seam, sear, seek, seem, seer, seme, sera, sere, skee

Federico Fellini

ceder, celli, cello, ceorl, cered, cider, cliff, cline, clone, coden, coder, coled, colin, coned, cored, credo, creed, creel, cried, crone, decor, defer, deice, dicer, diene, diner, dolce, dolci, donee, drill, droll, drone, edile, eerie, eider, elder, elfin, elide, eloin, ender, enrol, erode, felid, felon, fence, ficin, field, fiend, fifed, fifer, filed, filer, fille, fillo, fined, finer, fiord, fired, fleer, flied, flier, force, freed, fried, frill, frond, icier, idler, indie, indol, indri, infer, iodic, iodin, ionic, irone, leone, lifer, lined, liner, loden, loner, nerol, nicer, nicol, niece, offed, offer, oiled, oiler, olden, older, oldie, oleic, olein, orcin, oriel, recon, redon, refed, refel, relic, reoil, riced, ricin, rifle, riled, rille

Art Linkletter

aerie, airer, akene, alert, alien, alike, aline, allee, alter, anele, anile, ankle, antre, arete, ariel, artel, atilt, eaten, eater, elain, elate, elint, elite, enate, enter, entia, ileal, inert, inker, inkle, inlet, inter, irate, kerne, kiter, kneel, knell, knelt, krait, krill, laker, laree, laten, later, latke, leant, learn, liane, liken, liker, liner, liter, litre, niter, nitre, rakee, raker, ranee, ratel, rater, reink, relet, relit, renal, rente, reran, retia, retie, riant, rille, taint, taken, taker, takin, taler, tarre, tater, telae, telia, tenet, tenia, terai, terne, terra, tetra, tilak, tiler, tinea, titan, titer, title, titre, traik, trail, train, trait, trank, treat, treen, trial, trier, trike, trill, trine, trite

Alfred Nobel

abele, abler, abode, adobe, adore, adorn, afore, alder, aldol, allee, allod, alone, anele, anode, anole, ardeb, baled, baler, baned, barde, bared, baron, beano, beard, bedel, belle, blade, bland, blare, blear, bleed, blend, blond, board, bolar, boned, boner, boral, bored, borne, brand, bread, brede, breed, broad, debar, defer, dobla, dobra, donee, droll, drone, eared, eland, elder, ender, enrol, erode, fable, fader, fared, farle, fella, felon, feral, flare, fleer, flora, freed, frena, frond, label, labor, laden, lader, ladle, laree, learn, leben, leone, llano, lobar, lobed, loden, loner, loral, loran, naled, nerol, noble, nodal, oared, olden, older, orbed, oread, radon, ranee, rebel, redan, redon, refed, refel, renal, robed, roble

Goldie Hawn

adown, agile, aglow, agone, ahold, ailed, algid, algin, alien, align, aline, aloin, alone, along, angel, angle, anile, anode, anole, awing, awned, danio, dawen, deign, dewan, dhole, dinge, dingo, diwan, dogie, doing, donga, dowel, dowie, dwine, elain, eland, eloin, endow, gelid, genoa, geoid, glade, gland, glean, glide, gonad, gonia, gowan, haled, halid, haole, hawed, helio, hinge, hogan, holed, honda, honed, ideal, indol, indow, ingle, laden, laigh, lawed, liane, liang, ligan, lined, linga, lingo, loden, lodge, logan, logia, longe, lowed, naled, neigh, nidal, nodal, ogled, ohing, oiled, olden, oldie, olein, owing, owned, waged, wagon, waled, waned, weald, weigh, whale, whang, wheal, while, whine, whole, widen, wield, wigan, wiled, wined, woald, wodge

Amelia Earhart

aerie, aimer, airer, airth, alarm, alate, alert, almah, almeh, altar, alter, ameer, areae, areal, arete, arhat, ariel, armer, armet, artal, artel, atria, earth, eater, elate, elemi, elite, ether, haler, halma, hamal, harem, hater, heart, hemal, herma, hilar, hirer, ihram, irate, ither, laari, lahar, laith, lamer, lamia, laree, later, lathe, lathi, lethe, liter, lithe, litre, maile, malar, maria, mater, merer, merit, merle, metal, meter, metre, miler, mirth, miter, mitre, ramee, ramet, ramie, ratal, ratel, rater, rathe, realm, rearm, reata, rehem, relet, relit, remet, remit, retem, retia, retie, riata, rimer, talar, taler, tamal, tamer, tarre, telae, telia, terai, terra, tharm, their, theme, there, therm, thirl, three, tiara, tiler, timer, trail, trial, trier

Dianne Feinstein

adits, aedes, aides, anent, anise, anted, antes, antis, aside, dates, deans, deets, defat, defis, deist, denes, dense, dents, diene, diets, dines, dints, ditas, dites, eased, eaten, edits, enate, entia, etnas, fades, faint, fanes, fated, fates, fease, feast, feats, feeds, feint, feist, fends, fetas, feted, fetes, fetid, fiats, fiend, finds, fined, fines, finis, ideas, inane, indie, inned, inset, intis, naifs, nates, neats, needs, neifs, neist, nides, nines, nisei, nites, nitid, saint, saned, sated, satin, sedan, seine, senna, sente, senti, setae, sited, snide, stade, staid, stain, stand, stane, stead, steed, stein, stied, tains, tease, teens, teiid, teind, tends, tenia, tense, tides, tinea, tined, tines, tsade, tsadi

Milton Berle

belie, belle, beret, berme, betel, beton, biome, biont, birle, biter, blent, blite, boite, boner, borne, botel, brent, brill, brine, broil, brome, elemi, elint, elite, eloin, ember, emote, enorm, enrol, enter, inert, inlet, inter, intro, irone, leben, lemon, lento, leone, libel, liber, limbo, limen, liner, lirot, liter, litre, loner, melon, merit, merle, meter, metre, metro, miler, mille, miner, minor, miter, mitre, moire, monie, monte, morel, motel, nerol, niter, nitre, nitro, noble, noter, obeli, oiler, olein, omber, ombre, orbit, oriel, rebel, relet, relit, remet, remit, rente, reoil, retem, retie, rille, robin, roble, teloi, tenor, terne, tiler, timer, toile, toner, treen, tribe, trill, trine, triol, troll, trone

Margaret Thatcher

aargh, aceta, agama, agate, agree, ameer, areae, areca, arete, arhat, armer, armet, attar, cager, carat, carer, caret, carte, cater, chare, charm, charr, chart, cheat, cheer, chert, cheth, crate, cream, creme, eager, eagre, earth, eater, egret, erect, ether, gamer, garth, gerah, grace, grama, grate, great, greet, harem, hatch, hater, heart, heath, herma, macer, mache, march, marge, match, mater, matte, merer, merge, meter, metre, racer, ragee, ramee, ramet, rarer, ratch, rater, rathe, reach, react, rearm, reata, recta, regma, rehem, remet, retag, retch, retem, tacet, tache, tamer, targe, tarre, tatar, tater, teach, tecta, teeth, terce, terga, terra, tetra, tharm, theca, theme, there, therm, theta, three, trace, tract, treat

Regis Philbin

begin, being, bergs, biers, biles, bilge, bines, binge, birle, birls, birse, blini, blips, brens, bries, brigs, brine, bring, brins, genii, genip, giber, gibes, girls, girns, girsh, glens, grins, gripe, grips, heils, heirs, helps, herbs, herls, herns, hinge, hires, ingle, iring, lehrs, lenis, liber, libri, liens, liers, liger, liner, lines, lings, lipin, neigh, nighs, nihil, nisei, peins, penis, peril, peris, piers, piing, pilei, piles, pilis, pines, pings, pirns, plebs, plier, plies, pries, prigs, prise, reign, reins, renig, repin, resin, ribes, riels, riles, rings, rinse, ripen, ripes, risen, rishi, segni, sengi, serin, shiel, shier, shine, shire, shlep, sigil, singe, siren, slier, sling, slipe, snipe, speil, speir, spiel, spier, spile, spine, spire, sprig

Gerard Depardieu

adage, added, adder, adieu, aerie, agape, agree, agria, aided, aider, aired, airer, areae, argue, audad, auger, aurae, aurar, aurei, dared, darer, deair, direr, dirge, drape, dread, drear, dreed, dried, drier, druid, drupe, duded, duped, duper, dured, durra, eager, eagre, eared, edged, edger, eerie, eider, erred, gaddi, gadid, gaped, gaper, grade, grape, greed, gride, gripe, guard, guide, irade, padre, padri, paged, pager, pardi, pared, parer, pareu, parge, peage, perdu, perea, preed, pride, pried, prier, prude, purda, puree, purer, purge, radar, raged, ragee, raped, raper, rapid, rared, rarer, readd, reded, redia, redid, redip, repeg, rerig, rider, ridge, riped, riper, ruder, rugae, rupee, udder, uraei, urare, urari, urged, urger

Barry Manilow

aboil, aboma, alamo, alarm, alary, aliya, aloin, alway, amain, ambry, amino, amnia, anima, anomy, arbor, armor, aroma, array, arrow, bairn, balmy, banal, barmy, barny, baron, bialy, binal, blain, blawn, blimy, blown, blowy, bolar, boral, boyar, boyla, brail, brain, brawl, brawn, briar, briny, broil, brown, bwana, bylaw, inarm, inlay, irony, laari, labia, labor, labra, lamby, lamia, lanai, lawny, liana, libra, liman, limba, limbo, limby, loamy, lobar, loran, lorry, malar, mania, manly, manor, maria, marly, marry, mayan, mayor, mbira, miaow, minor, moira, molar, moral, moray, naira, nawab, nobly, noily, noria, noway, nyala, rainy, rawin, rawly, rayon, riyal, robin, roily, roman, rowan, royal, wanly, wirra, woman, womby, wormy, worry

Carrie Fisher

aches, acres, aerie, afire, airer, areic, arise, arris, cafes, carer, cares, carrs, carse, cease, ceres, ceria, chafe, chair, chare, charr, chars, chase, cheer, chefs, chias, chief, chirr, cires, cirri, crash, crier, cries, eches, erase, erica, escar, facer, faces, fairs, farce, farci, farer, fares, fears, fease, feces, feres, feria, fiars, fices, fiche, firer, fires, freer, frees, frere, fresh, friar, frier, fries, frise, hafis, hairs, hares, hears, heirs, heres, hirer, hires, icier, racer, races, raise, rarer, rares, raser, reach, rears, reefs, refer, reifs, rheas, ricer, rices, rifer, riser, rishi, safer, saice, saree, scare, scarf, scree, serac, serai, serer, serif, share, sheaf, shear, sheer, shier, shire, shirr, siree, sirra

Liam Neeson

aeons, aisle, alien, aline, almes, aloes, aloin, alone, amens, amies, amine, amino, amins, amole, anele, anile, anils, anime, anion, anise, anole, easel, elain, elans, elemi, eloin, enema, enols, eosin, inane, lames, lanes, leans, lease, leman, lemon, lenes, lenis, lenos, lense, leone, liane, liens, liman, limas, limen, limes, limns, limos, linen, lines, linns, linos, lions, loams, loans, loins, maile, mails, mains, males, manes, manos, manse, mason, meals, means, melon, mensa, mense, mesne, meson, miens, miles, milos, minae, minas, mines, moans, moils, molas, moles, monas, monie, nails, names, neems, nemas, neons, nines, noels, noils, noise, nomas, nomen, nomes, nonas, nones, olein, omens, salmi, salon, seine, semen, senna, slain, slime, smile, snail, solan, solei

Golda Meir

adore, agile, aider, ailed, aimed, aimer, aired, alder, algid, algor, amide, amido, amigo, amole, argil, argle, argol, ariel, armed, aroid, deair, derma, dimer, dirge, dogie, dogma, dolma, domal, drail, dream, gamed, gamer, gelid, geoid, gimel, glade, glair, glare, gleam, glide, glime, gloam, golem, goral, gored, grade, grail, gride, grime, ideal, idler, image, imago, irade, lader, lager, laird, lamed, lamer, large, largo, liard, lidar, liger, limed, lodge, logia, madre, maile, marge, medal, media, midge, miler, mired, modal, model, moira, moire, molar, morae, moral, morel, oared, ogled, ogler, oiled, oiler, older, oldie, omega, oread, oriel, radio, raged, ramie, realm, redia, regal, regma, reoil, ridge, riled, rimed

Dean Martin

adman, admen, admit, aider, aimed, aimer, aired, amain, amend, ament, amide, amine, amnia, anear, anent, anima, anime, antae, anted, antra, antre, arena, armed, armet, atman, atria, daman, damar, dater, deair, demit, denim, derat, derma, dimer, dinar, diner, drain, drama, dream, entia, inane, inarm, inert, inned, inner, inter, irade, irate, madre, maned, mania, manna, manta, maria, mated, mater, matin, meant, media, menad, menta, merit, minae, mined, miner, mired, miter, mitre, nadir, naiad, naira, named, namer, niter, nitre, ramet, ramie, ranid, ratan, rated, reata, redan, redia, reman, remit, renin, retia, riant, riata, rimed, tamed, tamer, tared, teind, tenia, terai, tiara, timed, timer, tinea, tined, tired, trade, train, tread, trend, triad, tried, trine

Frankie Valli

aalii, afire, aiver, akela, alane, alien, alike, aline, alive, anear, anile, ankle, anvil, areal, arena, ariel, arval, avail, avian, elain, elfin, ervil, faena, faker, fakir, farle, fella, feral, feria, filar, filer, fille, final, finer, fiver, flail, flair, flake, flank, flare, flier, frail, frank, freak, frena, frill, ileal, ilial, infer, infra, inker, inkle, invar, kafir, kalif, kefir, kenaf, kevil, knave, knell, knife, kraal, krill, laari, laker, lanai, larva, laver, learn, levin, liana, liane, lifer, liken, liker, liner, liven, liver, livre, naevi, naira, naive, naval, navar, navel, nival, ravel, raven, ravin, reink, renal, rifle, rille, rival, riven, vakil, varia, varna, velar, venal, viler, villa, villi, vinal, viral

Petula Clark

aceta, acute, akela, alack, alate, alert, altar, alter, alula, apace, apart, apeak, apter, areal, areca, artal, artel, aurae, aural, calla, caper, caput, carat, caret, carle, carte, cater, caulk, cella, clapt, clear, cleat, clept, clerk, craal, crake, crape, crate, creak, crept, cruel, cruet, culet, culpa, cupel, curet, cuter, eclat, epact, eruct, erupt, kalpa, kaput, karat, kraal, kraut, kurta, lacer, laker, lapel, later, latke, laura, leapt, lepta, letup, lucre, lutea, pacer, palea, paler, palet, pareu, parka, parle, pater, pearl, peart, petal, place, plack, plate, pleat, pluck, prate, pruta, pucka, puler, ratal, ratel, react, reata, recap, recta, recut, taker, talar, taler, taluk, taper, taupe, tepal, trace, track, truce, truck, trull, tulle, ulcer, ultra, urate, ureal

Kurt Cobain

abort, about, acorn, actin, actor, antic, auric, bacon, bairn, banco, baric, baron, batik, baton, biont, biota, boart, boric, bourn, bract, brain, brank, brant, brick, brink, brock, bronc, bruin, bruit, brunt, bucko, bunco, bunko, buran, burin, burnt, cabin, cairn, canto, carbo, carob, coati, cobia, cobra, coria, cornu, cotan, count, court, crank, croak, cubit, curia, curio, cutin, incur, intro, kauri, knaur, knout, korai, korat, korun, krait, kraut, krona, krubi, kurta, narco, naric, nitro, noria, nubia, octan, ontic, orbit, orcin, rabic, racon, ratio, riant, robin, runic, rutin, tabor, tabun, takin, taroc, tarok, tonic, toric, track, traik, train, trank, triac, trick, troak, trock, trona, truck, trunk, tunic, turbo, unbar, uncia, urban, urbia

Stephen King

egest, eight, eking, geeks, geest, genes, genet, genie, genip, gents, geste, ghees, ginks, heist, hents, hikes, hinge, hints, inept, inset, keens, keeps, keets, kepis, khets, kines, kings, kites, kithe, kiths, knees, knish, knits, neeps, neigh, neist, nighs, night, nines, ninth, nites, peeks, peens, peins, peise, pekes, pekin, penes, penis, penne, penni, pikes, pines, pings, pinks, pints, piste, piths, segni, seine, sengi, sente, senti, sheen, sheep, sheet, sheik, shent, shine, shtik, siege, sight, singe, skeen, skeet, skein, skene, skint, skite, snipe, spent, spike, spine, spite, steek, steep, stein, sting, stink, stipe, teens, tense, thegn, thein, thens, these, thine, thing, think, thins, tikes, tines, tinge, tings

Pablo Picasso

abaci, aboil, albas, alias, appal, apsis, aspic, aspis, assai, baals, bails, balas, balsa, basal, basic, basil, basis, bassi, basso, blips, bliss, blocs, bloop, boils, bolas, bolos, cabal, capos, casas, cibol, claps, clasp, class, clips, clops, coala, coals, cobia, coils, colas, cools, coops, copal, isbas, labia, laics, lapis, lasso, lisps, lobos, locos, loops, oasis, obias, oboli, obols, olios, opals, ossia, pacas, pails, paisa, palpi, palps, papal, papas, pibal, pical, picas, pipal, pisco, pisos, plica, plops, polio, polis, polos, pools, poops, psoai, psoas, sails, salic, salpa, salps, salsa, scabs, scalp, scoop, scops, sials, silos, sisal, slabs, slaps, slips, slobs, sloop, slops, soaps, soils, solos, spail, spica, spics, spoil, spool

Chapter 9: *Word Ladders*

These puzzles have many possible solutions. Here are some answers; yours might be different.

BOY to MAN

BOY, BAY, MAY, MAN

AIR to ART

AIR, AIM, ARM, ART

CAR to TOY

CAR, BAR, BAY, BOY, TOY

PIG to HAM

PIG, BIG, BAG, HAG, HAM

LOG to OAR

LOG, LAG, TAG, TAR, OAR

BEE to WAX

BEE, WEE, WED, WAD, WAX

FOX to DEN

FOX, FAX, FAN, PAN, PEN, DEN

EAT to ATE

EAT, BAT, BET, BEE, BYE, AYE, ATE

DOC to FLU

DOC, DOE, JOE, JOY, SOY, SLY, FLY, FLU

EGG TO HEN

EGG, EGO, AGO, AGE, AYE, BYE, BEE, TEE, TEN, HEN

TIME to BELL

TIME, TILE, TILL, TELL, BELL

SING to TONE

SING, DING, DINE, DONE, TONE

COAT to SHOE

COAT, BOAT, BOOT, SOOT, SHOT, SHOE

SEND to HOME

SEND, SAND, SANE, SAME, SOME, HOME

POND to LAKE

POND, BOND, BAND, LAND, LANE, LAKE

PLAY to GROW

PLAY, CLAY, CLAW, FLAW, FLOW, GLOW, GROW

BOOK to FILM

BOOK, COOK, CORK, FORK, FORM, FIRM, FILM

ZERO to FREE

ZERO, HERO, HERD, HEED, FEED, FEET, FRET, FREE

TOWN to CITY

TOWN, TORN, CORN, CORE, CURE, CUTE, CITE, CITY

KISS to TELL

KISS, KIDS, AIDS, AIDE, TIDE, TILE, TILL, TELL

SIREN to FADES

SIREN, SIRES, FIRES, FARES, FADES

PAPER to GAMES

PAPER, TAPER, TAMER, GAMER, GAMES

MOUSE to WORST

MOUSE, HOUSE, HORSE, WORSE, WORST

CLUMP to TRASH

CLUMP, CLAMP, CLASP, CLASH, CRASH, TRASH

START to PHONE

START, STARE, STORE, STONE, SHONE, PHONE

WATER to PALES

WATER, LATER, LAYER, PAYER, PALER, PALES

OUTER to BAKED

OUTER, CUTER, CURER, CURED, CARED, CAKED, BAKED

TIGER to MATED

TIGER, TIMER, TIMES, TILES, MILES, MALES, MATES, MATED

THE EVERYTHING SERIES!

BUSINESS & PERSONAL FINANCE

Everything® Accounting Book
Everything® Budgeting Book, 2nd Ed.
Everything® Business Planning Book
Everything® Coaching and Mentoring Book, 2nd Ed.
Everything® Fundraising Book
Everything® Get Out of Debt Book
Everything® Grant Writing Book, 2nd Ed.
Everything® Guide to Buying Foreclosures
Everything® Guide to Mortgages
Everything® Guide to Personal Finance for Single Mothers
Everything® Home-Based Business Book, 2nd Ed.
Everything® Homebuying Book, 2nd Ed.
Everything® Homeselling Book, 2nd Ed.
Everything® Human Resource Management Book
Everything® Improve Your Credit Book
Everything® Investing Book, 2nd Ed.
Everything® Landlording Book
Everything® Leadership Book, 2nd Ed.
Everything® Managing People Book, 2nd Ed.
Everything® Negotiating Book
Everything® Online Auctions Book
Everything® Online Business Book
Everything® Personal Finance Book
Everything® Personal Finance in Your 20s & 30s Book, 2nd Ed.
Everything® Project Management Book, 2nd Ed.
Everything® Real Estate Investing Book
Everything® Retirement Planning Book
Everything® Robert's Rules Book, $7.95
Everything® Selling Book
Everything® Start Your Own Business Book, 2nd Ed.
Everything® Wills & Estate Planning Book

COOKING

Everything® Barbecue Cookbook
Everything® Bartender's Book, 2nd Ed., $9.95
Everything® Calorie Counting Cookbook
Everything® Cheese Book
Everything® Chinese Cookbook
Everything® Classic Recipes Book
Everything® Cocktail Parties & Drinks Book
Everything® College Cookbook
Everything® Cooking for Baby and Toddler Book
Everything® Cooking for Two Cookbook
Everything® Diabetes Cookbook
Everything® Easy Gourmet Cookbook
Everything® Fondue Cookbook
Everything® Fondue Party Book
Everything® Gluten-Free Cookbook
Everything® Glycemic Index Cookbook
Everything® Grilling Cookbook
Everything® Healthy Meals in Minutes Cookbook
Everything® Holiday Cookbook
Everything® Indian Cookbook
Everything® Italian Cookbook

Everything® Lactose-Free Cookbook
Everything® Low-Carb Cookbook
Everything® Low-Cholesterol Cookbook
Everything® Low-Fat High-Flavor Cookbook
Everything® Low-Salt Cookbook
Everything® Meals for a Month Cookbook
Everything® Meals on a Budget Cookbook
Everything® Mediterranean Cookbook
Everything® Mexican Cookbook
Everything® No Trans Fat Cookbook
Everything® One-Pot Cookbook
Everything® Pizza Cookbook
Everything® Quick and Easy 30-Minute, 5-Ingredient Cookbook
Everything® Quick Meals Cookbook
Everything® Slow Cooker Cookbook
Everything® Slow Cooking for a Crowd Cookbook
Everything® Soup Cookbook
Everything® Stir-Fry Cookbook
Everything® Sugar-Free Cookbook
Everything® Tapas and Small Plates Cookbook
Everything® Tex-Mex Cookbook
Everything® Thai Cookbook
Everything® Vegetarian Cookbook
Everything® Whole-Grain, High-Fiber Cookbook
Everything® Wild Game Cookbook
Everything® Wine Book, 2nd Ed.

GAMES

Everything® 15-Minute Sudoku Book, $9.95
Everything® 30-Minute Sudoku Book, $9.95
Everything® Bible Crosswords Book, $9.95
Everything® Blackjack Strategy Book
Everything® Brain Strain Book, $9.95
Everything® Bridge Book
Everything® Card Games Book
Everything® Card Tricks Book, $9.95
Everything® Casino Gambling Book, 2nd Ed.
Everything® Chess Basics Book
Everything® Craps Strategy Book
Everything® Crossword and Puzzle Book
Everything® Crossword Challenge Book
Everything® Crosswords for the Beach Book, $9.95
Everything® Cryptic Crosswords Book, $9.95
Everything® Cryptograms Book, $9.95
Everything® Easy Crosswords Book
Everything® Easy Kakuro Book, $9.95
Everything® Easy Large-Print Crosswords Book
Everything® Games Book, 2nd Ed.
Everything® Giant Sudoku Book, $9.95
Everything® Giant Word Search Book
Everything® Kakuro Challenge Book, $9.95
Everything® Large-Print Crossword Challenge Book
Everything® Large-Print Crosswords Book
Everything® Lateral Thinking Puzzles Book, $9.95
Everything® Literary Crosswords Book, $9.95
Everything® Mazes Book
Everything® Memory Booster Puzzles Book, $9.95
Everything® Movie Crosswords Book, $9.95

Everything® Music Crosswords Book, $9.95
Everything® Online Poker Book
Everything® Pencil Puzzles Book, $9.95
Everything® Poker Strategy Book
Everything® Pool & Billiards Book
Everything® Puzzles for Commuters Book, $9.95
Everything® Puzzles for Dog Lovers Book, $9.95
Everything® Sports Crosswords Book, $9.95
Everything® Test Your IQ Book, $9.95
Everything® Texas Hold 'Em Book, $9.95
Everything® Travel Crosswords Book, $9.95
Everything® TV Crosswords Book, $9.95
Everything® Word Games Challenge Book
Everything® Word Scramble Book
Everything® Word Search Book

HEALTH

Everything® Alzheimer's Book
Everything® Diabetes Book
Everything® First Aid Book, $9.95
Everything® Health Guide to Adult Bipolar Disorder
Everything® Health Guide to Arthritis
Everything® Health Guide to Controlling Anxiety
Everything® Health Guide to Depression
Everything® Health Guide to Fibromyalgia
Everything® Health Guide to Menopause, 2nd Ed.
Everything® Health Guide to Migraines
Everything® Health Guide to OCD
Everything® Health Guide to PMS
Everything® Health Guide to Postpartum Care
Everything® Health Guide to Thyroid Disease
Everything® Hypnosis Book
Everything® Low Cholesterol Book
Everything® Menopause Book
Everything® Nutrition Book
Everything® Reflexology Book
Everything® Stress Management Book

HISTORY

Everything® American Government Book
Everything® American History Book, 2nd Ed.
Everything® Civil War Book
Everything® Freemasons Book
Everything® Irish History & Heritage Book
Everything® Middle East Book
Everything® World War II Book, 2nd Ed.

HOBBIES

Everything® Candlemaking Book
Everything® Cartooning Book
Everything® Coin Collecting Book
Everything® Digital Photography Book, 2nd Ed.
Everything® Drawing Book
Everything® Family Tree Book, 2nd Ed.
Everything® Knitting Book
Everything® Knots Book
Everything® Photography Book
Everything® Quilting Book

Everything® Sewing Book
Everything® Soapmaking Book, 2nd Ed.
Everything® Woodworking Book

HOME IMPROVEMENT

Everything® Feng Shui Book
Everything® Feng Shui Decluttering Book, $9.95
Everything® Fix-It Book
Everything® Green Living Book
Everything® Home Decorating Book
Everything® Home Storage Solutions Book
Everything® Homebuilding Book
Everything® Organize Your Home Book, 2nd Ed.

KIDS' BOOKS

All titles are $7.95

Everything® Fairy Tales Book, $14.95
Everything® Kids' Animal Puzzle & Activity Book
Everything® Kids' Astronomy Book
Everything® Kids' Baseball Book, 5th Ed.
Everything® Kids' Bible Trivia Book
Everything® Kids' Bugs Book
Everything® Kids' Cars and Trucks Puzzle and Activity Book
Everything® Kids' Christmas Puzzle & Activity Book
Everything® Kids' Connect the Dots Puzzle and Activity Book
Everything® Kids' Cookbook
Everything® Kids' Crazy Puzzles Book
Everything® Kids' Dinosaurs Book
Everything® Kids' Environment Book
Everything® Kids' Fairies Puzzle and Activity Book
Everything® Kids' First Spanish Puzzle and Activity Book
Everything® Kids' Football Book
Everything® Kids' Gross Cookbook
Everything® Kids' Gross Hidden Pictures Book
Everything® Kids' Gross Jokes Book
Everything® Kids' Gross Mazes Book
Everything® Kids' Gross Puzzle & Activity Book
Everything® Kids' Halloween Puzzle & Activity Book
Everything® Kids' Hidden Pictures Book
Everything® Kids' Horses Book
Everything® Kids' Joke Book
Everything® Kids' Knock Knock Book
Everything® Kids' Learning French Book
Everything® Kids' Learning Spanish Book
Everything® Kids' Magical Science Experiments Book
Everything® Kids' Math Puzzles Book
Everything® Kids' Mazes Book
Everything® Kids' Money Book
Everything® Kids' Nature Book
Everything® Kids' Pirates Puzzle and Activity Book
Everything® Kids' Presidents Book
Everything® Kids' Princess Puzzle and Activity Book
Everything® Kids' Puzzle Book
Everything® Kids' Racecars Puzzle and Activity Book
Everything® Kids' Riddles & Brain Teasers Book
Everything® Kids' Science Experiments Book
Everything® Kids' Sharks Book
Everything® Kids' Soccer Book
Everything® Kids' Spies Puzzle and Activity Book
Everything® Kids' States Book
Everything® Kids' Travel Activity Book
Everything® Kids' Word Search Puzzle and Activity Book

LANGUAGE

Everything® Conversational Japanese Book with CD, $19.95
Everything® French Grammar Book
Everything® French Phrase Book, $9.95
Everything® French Verb Book, $9.95
Everything® German Practice Book with CD, $19.95
Everything® Inglés Book
Everything® Intermediate Spanish Book with CD, $19.95
Everything® Italian Practice Book with CD, $19.95
Everything® Learning Brazilian Portuguese Book with CD, $19.95
Everything® Learning French Book with CD, 2nd Ed., $19.95
Everything® Learning German Book
Everything® Learning Italian Book
Everything® Learning Latin Book
Everything® Learning Russian Book with CD, $19.95
Everything® Learning Spanish Book
Everything® Learning Spanish Book with CD, 2nd Ed., $19.95
Everything® Russian Practice Book with CD, $19.95
Everything® Sign Language Book
Everything® Spanish Grammar Book
Everything® Spanish Phrase Book, $9.95
Everything® Spanish Practice Book with CD, $19.95
Everything® Spanish Verb Book, $9.95
Everything® Speaking Mandarin Chinese Book with CD, $19.95

MUSIC

Everything® Bass Guitar Book with CD, $19.95
Everything® Drums Book with CD, $19.95
Everything® Guitar Book with CD, 2nd Ed., $19.95
Everything® Guitar Chords Book with CD, $19.95
Everything® Harmonica Book with CD, $15.95
Everything® Home Recording Book
Everything® Music Theory Book with CD, $19.95
Everything® Reading Music Book with CD, $19.95
Everything® Rock & Blues Guitar Book with CD, $19.95
Everything® Rock & Blues Piano Book with CD, $19.95
Everything® Songwriting Book

NEW AGE

Everything® Astrology Book, 2nd Ed.
Everything® Birthday Personology Book
Everything® Dreams Book, 2nd Ed.
Everything® Love Signs Book, $9.95
Everything® Love Spells Book, $9.95
Everything® Paganism Book
Everything® Palmistry Book
Everything® Psychic Book
Everything® Reiki Book
Everything® Sex Signs Book, $9.95
Everything® Spells & Charms Book, 2nd Ed.
Everything® Tarot Book, 2nd Ed.
Everything® Toltec Wisdom Book
Everything® Wicca & Witchcraft Book, 2nd Ed.

PARENTING

Everything® Baby Names Book, 2nd Ed.
Everything® Baby Shower Book, 2nd Ed.
Everything® Baby Sign Language Book with DVD
Everything® Baby's First Year Book
Everything® Birthing Book

Everything® Breastfeeding Book
Everything® Father-to-Be Book
Everything® Father's First Year Book
Everything® Get Ready for Baby Book, 2nd Ed.
Everything® Get Your Baby to Sleep Book, $9.95
Everything® Getting Pregnant Book
Everything® Guide to Pregnancy Over 35
Everything® Guide to Raising a One-Year-Old
Everything® Guide to Raising a Two-Year-Old
Everything® Guide to Raising Adolescent Boys
Everything® Guide to Raising Adolescent Girls
Everything® Mother's First Year Book
Everything® Parent's Guide to Childhood Illnesses
Everything® Parent's Guide to Children and Divorce
Everything® Parent's Guide to Children with ADD/ADHD
Everything® Parent's Guide to Children with Asperger's Syndrome
Everything® Parent's Guide to Children with Asthma
Everything® Parent's Guide to Children with Autism
Everything® Parent's Guide to Children with Bipolar Disorder
Everything® Parent's Guide to Children with Depression
Everything® Parent's Guide to Children with Dyslexia
Everything® Parent's Guide to Children with Juvenile Diabetes
Everything® Parent's Guide to Positive Discipline
Everything® Parent's Guide to Raising a Successful Child
Everything® Parent's Guide to Raising Boys
Everything® Parent's Guide to Raising Girls
Everything® Parent's Guide to Raising Siblings
Everything® Parent's Guide to Sensory Integration Disorder
Everything® Parent's Guide to Tantrums
Everything® Parent's Guide to the Strong-Willed Child
Everything® Parenting a Teenager Book
Everything® Potty Training Book, $9.95
Everything® Pregnancy Book, 3rd Ed.
Everything® Pregnancy Fitness Book
Everything® Pregnancy Nutrition Book
Everything® Pregnancy Organizer, 2nd Ed., $16.95
Everything® Toddler Activities Book
Everything® Toddler Book
Everything® Tween Book
Everything® Twins, Triplets, and More Book

PETS

Everything® Aquarium Book
Everything® Boxer Book
Everything® Cat Book, 2nd Ed.
Everything® Chihuahua Book
Everything® Cooking for Dogs Book
Everything® Dachshund Book
Everything® Dog Book, 2nd Ed.
Everything® Dog Grooming Book
Everything® Dog Health Book
Everything® Dog Obedience Book
Everything® Dog Owner's Organizer, $16.95
Everything® Dog Training and Tricks Book
Everything® German Shepherd Book
Everything® Golden Retriever Book
Everything® Horse Book
Everything® Horse Care Book
Everything® Horseback Riding Book
Everything® Labrador Retriever Book
Everything® Poodle Book
Everything® Pug Book

Everything® Puppy Book
Everything® Rottweiler Book
Everything® Small Dogs Book
Everything® Tropical Fish Book
Everything® Yorkshire Terrier Book

REFERENCE

Everything® American Presidents Book
Everything® Blogging Book
Everything® Build Your Vocabulary Book, $9.95
Everything® Car Care Book
Everything® Classical Mythology Book
Everything® Da Vinci Book
Everything® Divorce Book
Everything® Einstein Book
Everything® Enneagram Book
Everything® Etiquette Book, 2nd Ed.
Everything® Guide to C. S. Lewis & Narnia
Everything® Guide to Edgar Allan Poe
Everything® Guide to Understanding Philosophy
Everything® Inventions and Patents Book
Everything® Jacqueline Kennedy Onassis Book
Everything® John F. Kennedy Book
Everything® Mafia Book
Everything® Martin Luther King Jr. Book
Everything® Philosophy Book
Everything® Pirates Book
Everything® Private Investigation Book
Everything® Psychology Book
Everything® Public Speaking Book, $9.95
Everything® Shakespeare Book, 2nd Ed.

RELIGION

Everything® Angels Book
Everything® Bible Book
Everything® Bible Study Book with CD, $19.95
Everything® Buddhism Book
Everything® Catholicism Book
Everything® Christianity Book
Everything® Gnostic Gospels Book
Everything® History of the Bible Book
Everything® Jesus Book
Everything® Jewish History & Heritage Book
Everything® Judaism Book
Everything® Kabbalah Book
Everything® Koran Book
Everything® Mary Book
Everything® Mary Magdalene Book
Everything® Prayer Book
Everything® Saints Book, 2nd Ed.
Everything® Torah Book
Everything® Understanding Islam Book
Everything® Women of the Bible Book
Everything® World's Religions Book

SCHOOL & CAREERS

Everything® Career Tests Book
Everything® College Major Test Book
Everything® College Survival Book, 2nd Ed.
Everything® Cover Letter Book, 2nd Ed.
Everything® Filmmaking Book
Everything® Get-a-Job Book, 2nd Ed.
Everything® Guide to Being a Paralegal
Everything® Guide to Being a Personal Trainer
Everything® Guide to Being a Real Estate Agent
Everything® Guide to Being a Sales Rep
Everything® Guide to Being an Event Planner
Everything® Guide to Careers in Health Care
Everything® Guide to Careers in Law Enforcement
Everything® Guide to Government Jobs
Everything® Guide to Starting and Running a Catering Business
Everything® Guide to Starting and Running a Restaurant
Everything® Job Interview Book, 2nd Ed.
Everything® New Nurse Book
Everything® New Teacher Book
Everything® Paying for College Book
Everything® Practice Interview Book
Everything® Resume Book, 3rd Ed.
Everything® Study Book

SELF-HELP

Everything® Body Language Book
Everything® Dating Book, 2nd Ed.
Everything® Great Sex Book
Everything® Self-Esteem Book
Everything® Tantric Sex Book

SPORTS & FITNESS

Everything® Easy Fitness Book
Everything® Fishing Book
Everything® Krav Maga for Fitness Book
Everything® Running Book, 2nd Ed.

TRAVEL

Everything® Family Guide to Coastal Florida
Everything® Family Guide to Cruise Vacations
Everything® Family Guide to Hawaii
Everything® Family Guide to Las Vegas, 2nd Ed.
Everything® Family Guide to Mexico
Everything® Family Guide to New England, 2nd Ed.
Everything® Family Guide to New York City, 3rd Ed.
Everything® Family Guide to RV Travel & Campgrounds
Everything® Family Guide to the Caribbean
Everything® Family Guide to the Disneyland® Resort, California Adventure®, Universal Studios®, and the Anaheim Area, 2nd Ed.
Everything® Family Guide to the Walt Disney World Resort®, Universal Studios®, and Greater Orlando, 5th Ed.
Everything® Family Guide to Timeshares
Everything® Family Guide to Washington D.C., 2nd Ed.

WEDDINGS

Everything® Bachelorette Party Book, $9.95
Everything® Bridesmaid Book, $9.95
Everything® Destination Wedding Book
Everything® Father of the Bride Book, $9.95
Everything® Groom Book, $9.95
Everything® Mother of the Bride Book, $9.95
Everything® Outdoor Wedding Book
Everything® Wedding Book, 3rd Ed.
Everything® Wedding Checklist, $9.95
Everything® Wedding Etiquette Book, $9.95
Everything® Wedding Organizer, 2nd Ed., $16.95
Everything® Wedding Shower Book, $9.95
Everything® Wedding Vows Book, $9.95
Everything® Wedding Workout Book
Everything® Weddings on a Budget Book, 2nd Ed., $9.95

WRITING

Everything® Creative Writing Book
Everything® Get Published Book, 2nd Ed.
Everything® Grammar and Style Book, 2nd Ed.
Everything® Guide to Magazine Writing
Everything® Guide to Writing a Book Proposal
Everything® Guide to Writing a Novel
Everything® Guide to Writing Children's Books
Everything® Guide to Writing Copy
Everything® Guide to Writing Graphic Novels
Everything® Guide to Writing Research Papers
Everything® Improve Your Writing Book, 2nd Ed.
Everything® Writing Poetry Book